THE GODLESS CONSTITUTION

A Moral Defense of the Secular State

THE
GODLESS
CONSTITUTION

A Moral Defense
of the Secular State

ISAAC KRAMNICK
and
R. LAURENCE MOORE

W. W. NORTON & COMPANY

NEW YORK / LONDON

For information about permission to reproduce selections from this book,
write to Permissions, W. W. Norton & Company, Inc., 500 Fifth Avenue, New York,
NY 10110.

Manufacturing by the Haddon Craftsmen, Inc.
Book design by JAM Design

The Library of Congress has cataloged the previous edition as follows:

Kramnick, Isaac.
The godless constitution: the case against religious correctness
/by Isaac Kramnick and R. Laurence Moore.
p. cm.
Includes bibliographical references and index.
1. Church and state—United States. 2. Freedom of religion—
United States. I. Moore, R. Laurence (Robert Laurence), 1940-
II. Title.
BR516.K73 1996
322' . 1'0973—dc20
95-20735

ISBN 0-393-32837-6

W. W. Norton & Company, Inc.
500 Fifth Avenue, New York, N. Y. 10110
www.wwnorton.com

W. W. Norton & Company Ltd.
Castle House, 75/76 Wells Street, London W1T 3QT

3 4 5 6 7 8 9 0

To Thomas Jefferson,
Roger Williams,
and
Their American Principles of Church and State

CONTENTS

CHAPTER ONE

IS AMERICA
A CHRISTIAN NATION?

AMERICANS SEEM TO fight about many silly things: whether a copy of the Ten Commandments can be posted in a city courthouse; whether a holiday display that puts an image of the baby Jesus next to one of Frosty the Snowman violates the Constitution; whether fidgeting grade-schoolers may stand for a minute in silent "spiritual" meditation before classes begin. Common sense might suggest that these are harmless practices whose actual damage is to trivialize religion. Otherwise they threaten no one. Not children, who ignore them as the incomprehensible designs of absurd grown-ups. Not atheists, who may find them hypocritical and vulgar but hardly intimidating. Not Buddhists and Muslims, who in these small areas of daily practice can demand equal access to the public landscape. So why do they raise ideological storms?

The answer lies in what history has done to us. Some Americans have inherited extravagant hopes about what religion, specifically Christianity, may accomplish in solving social problems through moral instruction. Others look to a different legacy, one that suggests how easily partisan religion in the hands of a purported majority can become a dangerous form of intellectual and political tyranny. Both groups have become masters of hyperbolic language. However, their quarrels are not about nothing. If Americans have learned to make constitutional mountains out of religious molehills, it is because crucial principles may become endangered. The crèche or the menorah on public property becomes the nose of the camel sneaking into the tent where Americans have carefully enshrined the constitutional separation of church and state.

Should we be worried? The answer given in this book is yes, at least with respect to one area of ongoing controversy. The authors are concerned about current pronouncements made by politically charged religious activists, what is called in journalistic parlance the religious right. Their crusade is an old one. Now a prime target is abortion clinics. Before it was mail delivery on Sundays, or Catholic immigrants, or Darwinian biology in school curriculums. Whenever religion of any kind casts itself as the one true faith and starts trying to arrange public policy accordingly, people who believe that they have a stake in free institutions, whatever else might divide them politically, had better look out.

What follows, then, is a polemic. Since before the founding of the United States, European colonists in North America were arguing about the role of religion in public and political life. Broadly speaking, two distinct traditions exist. We intend to lay out the case for one of them—what we call the party of the godless Constitution and of godless politics. In brief, this position recognizes that the nation's founders, both in writing the Constitution and in defending it in the ratification debates, sought to separate the operations of government from any claim that human beings can know and follow divine direction in reaching policy decisions. They did this despite their enormous respect for religion, their faith in divinely endowed human rights, and their belief that democracy benefited from a moral citizenry who believed in God.

The party we defend is based on a crucial intellectual connection, derived historically from both religious and secular thinkers, between a godless Constitution and a God-fearing people.

We will call the other side in this debate that runs through American history the party of religious correctness. It maintains that the United States was established as a Christian nation by Christian people, with the Christian religion assigned a central place in guiding the nation's destiny. For those who adhered to this party in the past, it followed that politicians and laws had to pass the test of furthering someone's definition of a Christian public order. Recently some who belong to this party have suggested that the stress upon "Christian" be downplayed in their political pronouncements. By referring more ecumenically to the United States as a religious nation, they invite other religious traditions to join a family-values crusade launched originally by a particular form of Christian faith. However, whether the present-day religious right has really moved beyond earlier pronouncements suggesting the forms of American government can be entrusted only with a Christian people is, with respect to the issues raised in this book, beside the point. A shift in rhetorical strategy to widen political appeal does not affect the substantive issues at stake.

The label "religious correctness" is pejorative and is obviously intended to turn the tables on those who imagine that the only danger to our free political institutions lies in something they, pejoratively, call political correctness. Still, it is usefully descriptive. The two parties we designate both have plenty of historical legitimacy behind them. Our intent is not to prove that the tradition we oppose never existed in the mind of any respectable or learned American. Nor is it to demonstrate that our party has been universally composed of farsighted geniuses who have battled mean-spirited ignoramuses. Some proponents of religious correctness are misinformed and cynically manipulative. Some on the other side, our side, are arrogant and condescending. Most on both sides speak for points of view that have had large and articulate followings.

Important issues are at stake. We believe, we believe passionately, that the party of religious correctness represents an approach to public policy that is damaging—damaging to the American Constitution, damaging to political debate, and damaging to American children whose social and educational needs are seriously misstated by the programs of religious correctness. We argue with some confidence because over the long years of American history the party of religious correctness has lost most of the major wars. It lost because it was wrong, not because Americans despise religion.

The authors both recognize that religion is important in American life. We are sympathetic in broad terms with Stephen Carter's position, articulated in his *Culture of Disbelief,* that there is a difference between reinforcing Jefferson's wall of separation between church and state and seeking to silence any expression of religious values in public life. Granted, this difference is notoriously difficult to define in many specific disputes that come before the courts. We do not in this book attempt to settle the judicial controversies that rage over the religious clauses of the First Amendment. The extensive attention given to these judicial debates has tended to obscure the more general theme that is the concern of this book: that is, the intentionally secular base on which the Constitution was placed. However, since we will make reference to some First Amendment issues that have been politicized, it's worth noting that we both recognize that if Americans want to honor Thomas Jefferson, the first thing they must guard against in interpreting his famous metaphor of the wall of separation is overzealousness.

Thus, while neither author favors classroom prayer, however nonsectarian, in the public schools—because if the First Amendment means anything, it means that government should not sponsor or encourage a particular form of religious expression—neither views the issue as one of the burning social dilemmas of our time. The heated debate declaiming the damage on the one side and the benefits on the other is ludicrously overstated. So is the general debate about tax money for parochial schools. Both authors favor *allowing,* not requiring, local school districts to vote aid to parochial schools for the courses they teach that follow the curriculum of other certified schools. Among other benefits, it will help eliminate the category of politicians who make political capital out of purported religious hurts. Faith-driven politics is able to do the worst damage to America's political agenda when anyone can plausibly claim that government is going out of its way to put religion at a disadvantage. As will appear, the authors will be happy when religion has the same rights in the public sphere as General Motors, no more and no less.

So let us be as clear as we can be at the outset. We are aware of the crucial role that religion played in America's revolutionary struggle, of the importance that many Constitution makers attached to it, and of the energy it gave to many American crusades for social justice. We both in fact have written about these points. Our attitudes toward the proper and improper roles of religion in contemporary public life is a subject we will take up fully in the last chapter, after we have laid out the historical antecedents for our party's point of view. Suffice it to say that our intention is not to marginalize religion. If anything, it is to warn against the ways that some aggressive proponents of religious correctness are doing exactly that in their political battles, even as they try to lay the blame elsewhere.

Americans are a people who like to argue about their origins. We think that if we could just get straight what the founding fathers really thought, we might do everything right. This is an illusion. However, there are far worse intellectual exercises than arguing about the founding fathers. They were uncommonly bright people. One problem, however, is that Washington, Jefferson, and Madison said a variety of things. A handy quotation plucked from this or that letter can serve a lot of partisan causes. It is not the purpose of this project to prove that all the founding fathers would agree with everything we say. Nonetheless, a little attention to a few hard facts can clear away phony arguments on both sides.

For example, the endlessly repeated claim that the Americans of 1776 were a devoutly religious and especially Christian people, that in the words of Governor Kirk Fordice of Mississippi "the early days of this Union . . . were totally based on not only religion, but one particular religion—the Christian religion," is nonsense. It is of the same order as fanciful assertions made at the other extreme that none of the founders took God seriously. You can do many spins on Jefferson. But you cannot turn him into a Protestant evangelical who believed that Christianity was the only basis for moral systems, that only Bible-based ethics taught people the difference between right and wrong and showed them how to be good citizens in a democratic republic. Jefferson was certainly interested in the Bible and wrote about it. However, he was equally interested in, and better informed about, the classical moral philosophers of Greek and Rome who predated the Christian era. His famous Declaration of Independence invoked "the Laws of Nature and of Nature's God," a phrase that avoided particular Christian reference. Jefferson's God spoke to men and women through nature rather than through scriptural revelation. In the Declaration's long list of complaints against the English crown, not one was about religion.

Some of the founding fathers fretted that Americans weren't much interested in religion and most definitely weren't securely Christian. They had reason to be concerned. Although some versions of our national myths tell us that the English colonists to

North America were more religious than the people who stayed behind in England, that they carried Christian crosses ashore, fell on their knees, and dedicated themselves to the Christian God, the fact is that most English Protestants acted in these matters with less fervor than Spanish and French Catholics who had preceded them into many parts of the New World. In the middle of the seventeenth century many more zealous Puritans lived in London than in New England. And run-of-the-mill Anglicans, who always outnumbered Puritans in the American colonies during the seventeenth and eighteenth centuries, tended to be lazy church organizers, especially indifferent in the Carolinas, Virginia, and Georgia to the problems of staffing outlying parishes with competent clerics.

It is no surprise, then, that Americans in the era of the Revolution were a distinctly unchurched people. The highest estimates for the late eighteenth century make only about 10–15 percent of the population church members. The proportion varied from locale to locale, but Hector St. John de Crèvecoeur, the French visitor to America, had ample evidence to justify his observation that "religious indifference is imperceptibly disseminated from one end of the continent to the other." Churches would have been almost completely empty had it not been for women who were there largely because they could not participate in the political business of the Continental Congress and other secular arenas of public disputation. So much, then, for the claim of the television evangelist D. James Kennedy, who cited the small American Jewish population of 1776 as proof that the United States was intended to be "a Christian nation." It is not that early Americans were by the standards of the day particularly irreligious. In a general way most of them were Christian. Certainly they were not Muslim or Buddhist. However, Americans in 1776 had a long way to go before making themselves strongly Christian or strongly anything else relating to a religious persuasion.

The figure of church affiliation has gone up dramatically since the early years of the Republic. To be sure, if we are to judge from the biblical literacy of Americans (in a recent poll fewer than half could name one of the four Gospels), the doctrinal investment of most Americans in organized religion is light. Yet that is scarcely the result of a secularist-led conspiracy. Christian churches, in fact, have no cause to complain about their public visibility. In numerical terms they are doing as well as or better than anything else that engages Americans' interest and energy. Professional sports is possibly a close competitor among men. Politics for either sex is not. These days dire warnings about the marginalization of religion come usually from the religious right. How seriously can we take such warnings if the religious right can claim anywhere near the constituency that its literature boasts, about a quarter of the American voting population—24 million Protestant evangelicals and a large proportion of America's 58 million Catholics? Most groups would relish marginalization of that sort.

The truly curious thing about some of the complaints from the Christian Coalition, the most vocal group of religious activists on the scene today, is that the last two Democratic presidents in this county, Jimmy Carter and Bill Clinton, have been Bible-quoting Southern Baptists. Rather than welcoming them as spiritual allies, the Christian Coalition has turned to far more dubious men of faith: Ronald Reagan, whose odd California blend of Armageddon prophecy, astrology, and un-family values was largely indifferent to church institutions; and George H. Bush, who manipulated his old-line Episcopalian faith so weirdly to serve political opportunism that even the Christian Coalition blushed.

Ralph Reed, the director of the Christian Coalition, who has lately been hard at work to organize a religious voting bloc, wants to uproot Protestant fundamentalism from its formerly narrow ethos, which was hostile to Catholics and Jews. Much of what he says we can agree with. When he writes that "people of faith have a right to be heard, and their religion should not disqualify them from serving in office or participating in the political party of their choice," he makes perfect sense. However, he risks becoming disingenuous when he adds that the Christian Coalition in asking people to subscribe to its public policy views is not asking them to subscribe to its theology. Perhaps when Reed declares that religious conservatives do not want a "Christian" nation, he means that Christianity will never be made an established religion. Yet, given the evangelical Christian commitment to converting the heathen, a lot of what is said in the name of Christian politics easily becomes troubling to non-Christians. In any case, too much rhetoric emerging from the Christian Coalition suggests that disclaimers about the goal of a Christian nation amount to hedging bordering on hypocrisy. The issue is not whether a Christian church is tax supported. The issue is whether Christian faith is de facto a religious test for high political office.

When Reed, who has a Ph.D. degree in history, turns to the past, he asks us to admire the people who once called America a Christian nation. These examples are not irrelevant to the present climate of religious politics. The implication is always that only Christians and other religious people who agree with Christians (why otherwise retain the label Christian Coalition?) care about strong families and basic goodness. Only a party of religious correctness committed to a religious perspective that separates decent Americans from people who believe that a moral case can be made for abortion passes muster. When the political Christians of Texas took over the state Republican party, they defeated a resolution stating, "The Republican party is not a church. . . . A Republican should never be put in the position of having to defend or explain his faith in order to participate in the party process." Within the party of religious correctness, such a proposal amounts to intentional heresy.

We hear with little sympathy the complaints about the satirical abuse heaped upon many religious leaders who have ventured into the arena of political debate. To be sure, they have been lampooned. H. L. Mencken was not the first person to satirize religion and biblical literalism. Nor was Tom Paine, one of our revolutionary heroes, although he was especially good at it. Many jabs at the religious right are cheap shots. But cheap shots make up much of what in America passes for political debate. For ourselves, we would like to see that whole arena cleansed of what Republican elephants and Democratic donkeys leave behind. But we will not in these pages indulge in that utopian fantasy. Religious leaders who enter politics can demand no more than the same treatment accorded to business leaders, hot dog vendors, and jubilant proponents of a "Queer America." That's the liberalism of free expression that all Americans supposedly profess. If you want to go public with your opinions, then someone is going to judge you a moron. And there is always the risk that you may be. The First Amendment offers no protection against being wrong.

Many religious people keep their opinions to themselves and don't proselytize. That policy isn't the prescription here. American society especially invites a religious perspective in public debate. We only observe that if you want respect for your ideas, you have to earn it. As many members of the party of religious correctness note, Martin Luther King Jr. and Father Daniel Berrigan used religion to further what are viewed as left-leaning reform protests. Many people who attack Pat Robertson admire King and Berrigan. They once sent generous donations to the Southern Christian Leadership Conference. Are these people incapable of being consistent? That is a question that we certainly must address. We simply note now that neither King nor Berrigan escaped savage criticism for his actions. One of them went to jail. And the other was killed. Before anyone tries to wear the halo of martyrdom, he or she had better consider carefully the relative weight of the grievance.

Ralph Reed likes to quote Alexis de Tocqueville on religion's central place in American democratic society. The quotations are not always accurate, but he is right about one important thing. Tocqueville, like Benjamin Franklin, believed that religion is essential to the health of republican liberty. However, Reed apparently closed the pages of *Democracy in America* too soon. Had he read further, he would not have missed Tocqueville's point that it is dangerous for religion to tie itself to political institutions and to topical political controversy. Religion's considerable influence, Tocqueville insisted, lies in directing "the customs of the community" and in "regulating domestic life." Involvement in political debate about partisan issues is death to this mission. Tocqueville's reasoning was simple and very much to our point. "Agitation and mutability are inherent in the nature of democratic republics." Political wisdom changes overnight as Americans change their president every four years and their legislature every two years. If religion were to throw itself into this fray, "where could it take firm hold in the ebb and flow of human opinions? Where would be that respect which belongs to it, amid the struggles of faction? And what would become of its immortality, in the midst of universal decay?"

If Tocqueville is correct, and we think he is, then any effective marginalization of religion in public life cannot be blamed on people who are hostile to religion. Any such marginalization that may be part of our times has just as much been caused by those who would have us think that religious leaders who witnessed for their faith over the long course of history, who struggled and suffered, did so that we may know how to vote on a balanced-budget amendment, a plan to reform health insurance, or a proposal to deny welfare payments to teenage unmarried mothers. Such friends of faith measure the power of religion by how many votes are delivered to private lobby groups. They make the work of dime store atheists ridiculously simple.

Before Tocqueville many of this country's founding fathers knew that "agitation and mutability" were the stuff of democratic politics and that religion had best stay away from the insincere pandering of political speeches, the unbelievable nastiness of party newspapers, and all the posturing that drove "the struggles of faction" if it were to maintain respect and influence. While many at the birth of America advocated a Christian politics, the principal architects of our national government envisioned a godless Constitution and a godless politics. One would never know this, however, by listening to the Christian right today, which has an utterly different take on the American past.

Pat Robertson, one prominent spokesman for the Christian right, insists that America was founded as a Christian polity, which persisted until subverted by a cabal of twentieth-century liberals and freethinkers who replaced it with an un-American secular state. The rhetoric of the Christian right repeatedly calls for a return to America's lost Christianhood, as shaped by its founders. Ralph Reed proclaimed, before political realities modified his tone, that "what Christians have got to do is to take back this country" and "make it a country once again governed by Christians." Pat Robertson uses the same imagery of return. "If Christian people work together," he urges, "they can succeed during this decade in winning back control of the institutions that have been taken from them over the past 70 years."

America's original founding as a Christian state is central to the Christian right's conspiratorial theory of American history. The Dallas Baptist minister who delivered the benediction at the Republican National Convention in 1984 insists "that there is no such thing as separation of church and state. It is merely a figment of the imagination of infidels." The founder and president of the religious right's Rutherford Institute writes that "it's of little surprise then that . . . the entire Constitution was written to promote a Christian order." One of the Christian right's most visible spokesmen, the evangelist-psychologist James Dobson, distributes through his organization Focus on the Family a set of history lessons that seeks to show that "the concept of a secular state was virtually non-existent in 1776 as well as in 1787, when the Constitution was written, and no less so when the Bill of Rights was adopted. To read the Constitution as the charter for a secular state is to misread history. . . . The Constitution was designed to perpetuate a Christian order." Many of America's disorders, Dobson argues, stem from abandoning this unity of state and church. "This really was a Christian nation," he claims, "and, as far as its founders were concerned, to try separating Christianity from government is virtually impossible and would result in unthinkable damage to the nation and its people. Much of the damage we see around us must be attributed to this separation."

This reading of the mind of the men who wrote the godless Constitution is wrong. The principal framers of the American political system wanted no religious parties in national politics. They crafted a constitutional order that intended to make a person's religious convictions, or his lack of religious convictions, irrelevant in judging the value of his political opinion or in assessing his qualifications to hold political office. As we shall see, they were not quite able to do that. Otherwise, we would not be writing a book that concedes the existence of a strong countertradition that also dates back to the founders and that has had many able defenders. Yet, so successful were the drafters of the Constitution in defining government in secular terms that one of the most powerful criticisms of the Constitution when ratified and for succeeding decades was that it was indifferent to Christianity and God. It was denounced by many as a godless document, which is precisely what it is.

Those who crafted American national government as a secular institution called upon two traditions. They used the strong vision of separate spiritual and worldly realms found in the American religious thought of Roger Williams and the Baptists of the founding era. They also enlisted the English liberal tradition, which put at the center of its political philosophy individuals free of government, enjoying property and thinking and praying as they wished. From these two sources came America's Constitution in 1787, today still our fundamental law. Pat Robertson may think, as he claimed in 1993, that the wall of separation between church and state is "a lie of the left" and that "there is no such thing in the Constitution." History and victories won through the course of our American past tell us that he is wrong.

The paradox we confront in telling our story is the one we mentioned in the beginning. The creation of a godless constitution was not an act of irreverence. Far from it. It was an act of confidence in religion. It intended to let religion do what it did best, to preserve the civil morality necessary to democracy, without laying upon it the burdens of being tied to the fortunes of this or that political faction. The godless Constitution must be understood as part of the American system of voluntary church support that has proved itself a much greater boon to the fortunes of organized religion than the prior systems of church establishment ever were.

The argument of the book proceeds in the following way. Chapter 2 reviews the central arguments that were made for and against the godless Constitution in the late eighteenth century. In the next three chapters we follow the religious and secular sources that provided the proponents of the godless Constitution with their winning arguments. Roger Williams, John Locke, and Thomas Jefferson are the key figures. In Chapter 6 we turn to the fortunes of American Baptists, who have had a powerful influence on American attitudes toward religion and politics from the colonial period to the present. This chapter moves the story beyond the period of the writing of the Constitution. So does Chapter 7, which treats what proved to be defining episodes in the American history of church-state relations—the Sunday mail controversy and efforts to adopt a Christian amendment to the Constitution. In the final chapter we survey the contemporary contours of the heated controversy between the proponents of the godless Constitution and the proponents of religious correctness. In that chapter, and doubtless elsewhere, we allow ourselves an editorial voice. We trust, however, that by then the voice will have been earned and will seem as something other than a volley of cheap shots. One of the authors grew up in an Orthodox Jewish home. The other is descended from Irish and German Catholics on his mother's side and Calvinist Protestants on his father's. They write with a deep respect for America's religious traditions, traditions that prescribe tolerance but also the obligation to offer sharp dissent from whatever opinions and practices seem wrong and unjust.

CHAPTER TWO

THE GODLESS CONSTITUTION

AMERICANS REVERE THE CONSTITUTION. Drafted in Philadelphia in the summer of 1787, the Constitution stands with the flag as a symbol of national unity. America has no royal family, no heritage of timeless and integrative state institutions and symbols, no national church. Add to that America's history of being peopled by diverse religious, national, and racial stocks, many of whom came, or were brought here, long after the founding, and one can see how the Constitution could become such a focus of national identity and loyalty. There is precious little else to compete with it as a unifying and symbolic evocation of America. To this day, in fact, to become an American citizen it is traditional for immigrants to have to pass a test on the Constitution. Unlike the American flag, however, which has changed dramatically over the years, with the ever expanding number of states, the Constitution has endured virtually unchanged over two hundred years. This is, surely, another important source of its status as the focus of American identity—its stability and unchanging quality.

The U.S. Constitution is a strikingly spare document with but seven articles. Its very leanness suggested to contemporaries that they had produced a unique and metahistoric achievement. John Adams described it as "if not the greatest exertion of human understanding, [then] the greatest single effort of national deliberation that the world has ever seen." Foreigners have echoed this sentiment. On the Constitution's centennial in 1887 the English statesman William Gladstone contended that it "was the most wonderful work ever struck off at a given time by the brain and purpose of man."

Not only is that same Constitution (with its later amendments) still revered in America; it still functions repeatedly as a touchstone in debates about contemporary legislation and public policy—as it should. The views of the framers as codified in their Olympian document are constantly invoked and given respect in discussions of matters as diverse as gun control, budgets, and welfare reform. In no area of public debate is this more evident than in the issues of religion and politics. Americans are continually told that the framers were deeply religious, God-fearing Christians who, as Newt Gingrich likes to note, would, as Jefferson did, often integrate into their political prose pious phrases like " 'upon the altar of God' I proclaim this or that." It follows that such religious men drafted a Christian Constitution in which God presides over and inspires a Christian political system. "The Constitution was designed to perpetuate a Christian order," the Christian right's Focus on the Family informs us.

That's not what happened in 1787. God and Christianity are nowhere to be found in the American Constitution, a reality that infuriated many at the time. The U.S. Constitution, drafted in 1787 and ratified in 1788, is a godless document. Its utter neglect of religion was no oversight; it was apparent to all. Self-consciously designed to be an instrument with which to structure the secular politics of individual interest and happiness, the Constitution was bitterly attacked for its failure to mention God or

Christianity. Our history books usually describe in great detail the major arguments made against the federal Constitution by its Anti-Federalist opponents: it meant death to the states and introduced an elitist Senate and a monarchical presidency. They seldom mention, however, the concerted campaign to discredit the Constitution as irreligious, which for many of its opponents was its principal flaw. It is as if recognizing the dimension of this criticism would draw too much attention to what was being attacked—the secularism of the Constitution. In fact, this underdocumented and underremembered controversy of 1787–88 over the godless Constitution was one of the most important public debates ever held in America over the place of religion in politics. The advocates of a secular state won, and it is their Constitution we revere today.

Their advocacy overturned a host of precedents. Jefferson's Declaration of Independence has famously invoked the "Creator" in laying out the human rights that propelled the colonists into revolt against England. The Articles of Confederation of 1776, America's first framework of government, gave credit to "the Great Governor of the World," and most of the earliest state constitutions contained an explicit acknowledgment of God and of the relationship of Christianity to civil order. The Massachusetts state constitution of 1780, for example, contains in Article 2 the injunction "It is the duty of all men in society publicly and at stated seasons to worship the Supreme Being, the great Creator and Preserver of the universe." The U.S. Constitution of 1787, however, contains no mention of "God," the "Great Governor," "Creator and Preserver," or "Supreme Being" whatsoever. God is nowhere to be found in the Constitution, which also has nothing to say about the social value of Christian belief or about the importance of religion for a moral public life. Alongside its utter silence with respect to God and to the United States as a Christian nation, the Constitution's sole reference to religion made matters worse, only adding insult to injury. Article 6 declares that "no religious test shall ever be required as a qualification to any office or public trust under the United States." It was this provision that served as the textual focus for the great debate on religion and the Constitution at the founding.

While passionately debated in the new nation, the "no religious test" clause elicited surprisingly little discussion at the Philadelphia Constitutional Convention itself. It was introduced by Charles Pinckney, the governor of South Carolina, on August 20, whereupon it was referred immediately to the Committee on Detail without any debate among the delegates. The committee presented its general report on August 30 and made no reference to Pinckney's proposal. Not to be ignored, Pinckney moved it again from the convention floor. Roger Sherman of Connecticut, the committee chairman, held that the prohibition was "unnecessary," the prevailing "liberality" being a sufficient security against such tests. Gouverneur Morris and General Charles Cotesworth Pinckney seconded Governor Pinckney's motion, however. It was then voted on and, according to the Maryland delegate Luther Martin, "adopted by a very great majority of the convention, and without much debate." No records exist of the exact vote, but Madison's personal notes of the convention report that North Carolina voted no and that Maryland was divided. According to Luther Martin, "there were some members *so unfashionable* [his italics] as to think that a *belief in the existence of a Deity* and of a *state of future rewards and punishments* would be some security for the good conduct of our rulers, and that in a Christian country it would be at *least decent* to hold out some distinction between the professors of Christianity and downright infidelity or paganism."

Well might these "unfashionable" members be surprised at the position taken so easily by the majority at the Constitutional Convention, for eleven of the thirteen states had religious tests for public offices in their constitutions in 1787. Even in Rhode Island, once the most religiously pluralistic and liberal state, where small numbers of Catholics and Jews freely worshiped, only Protestants could vote or hold office. New Hampshire, New Jersey, both Carolinas, Vermont, and Georgia also required officials to be Protestants. Massachusetts and Maryland insisted on belief in the Christian religion as a qualification for office. Pennsylvania required its officials to be Protestants who believed in God and the divine inspiration of the Old and New Testaments; in Delaware all elected and appointed public officials were required to profess "faith in God the Father, and in Jesus Christ His only son, and in the Holy Ghost, one God blessed forevermore." Several state constitutions also required officeholders to acknowledge that God was a "rewarder of the good and punisher of the wicked."

Not that there weren't voices in the states opposing religious tests. The Catholic John Carroll of Maryland noted acerbically in 1787 that even as many state constitutions had been drafted in 1776 reserving public office to Protestants, "the American army swarmed with Roman Catholic soldiers." People of all faiths fought in the Revolution, he noted, assuming that they would not be "shackled by religious tests" and would be "entitled to a participation in the common blessings which crowned their efforts" once they returned to their states. Jews in Pennsylvania petitioned the state government in 1783 and 1787 to remove the requirement that officeholders be Protestants and believers in the New Testament, since it "deprives the Jews of the most eminent right of freemen." In Gorham, Massachusetts (now Maine), the inhabitants instructed their delegates to the Massachusetts constitutional convention of 1779 "that no restriction be required of any officer or ruler but merit, viz. a sufficient knowledge and understanding in matters relative to the office, and fidelity and firmness in the cause of Liberty." The Gorham delegates were unsuccessful in Boston.

The two exceptions among the state constitutions were those of Virginia and New York. In the former, Madison's and Jefferson's "Statute for Religious Freedom," passed in 1786, specified that no religious test could be applied to the holding of public office. Even more interesting was New York's constitution, which in 1777 self-consciously repudiated tests that sought to maintain "any particular denomination of Christians." The absence of religious tests would, the New York constitution claimed, "guard against that spiritual oppression and intolerance wherewith the bigotry and ambition of weak and wicked priests and princes have scourged mankind."

In Philadelphia the principles of Virginia and New York were written into the new federal Constitution "without much debate," reflecting perhaps the towering influence Madison and Hamilton had at the Constitutional Convention. New York's Hamilton had, in fact, earlier given Virginia's Madison his draft for a constitution, which included the clause "nor shall any religious test for any office or place, be ever established by law." As for Madison's views in 1787 on religion and politics, we have the evidence of his contributions to the *Federalist* papers, written by him, Hamilton, and John Jay in 1787 and 1788 to persuade New York state delegates to ratify the Constitution at their convention. These essays seldom mention God. (Newt Gingrich, so convinced that the *Federalist* papers are the final word on American politics that he urged all the members of the House of Representatives to read them when he became Speaker, must realize that nowhere do they discuss America as a Christian people with a Christian government.) Indeed, the one extended reference in the *Federalist* papers to religion, written by Madison, totally undercuts its value as a governmental means to promote civic virtue. In the famous *Federalist* No. 10 Madison argues that zealous pursuit of religious opinions, far from leading men to "cooperate for their common good," causes them to hate each other and disposes them "to vex and oppress each other."

If there was little debate in Philadelphia over the "no religious test" clause, a veritable firestorm broke out in the country at large during the ratification conventions in each of the states. Outraged Protestants attacked what they saw, correctly, as a godless Constitution. The "no religious test" clause was perceived by many to be the gravest defect of the Constitution. Colonel Jones, a Massachusetts delegate, told the state's ratifying convention that American political leaders had to believe in God and Jesus Christ. Amos Singletary, another delegate to the Massachusetts ratification convention, was upset at the Constitution's not requiring men in power to be religious "and though he hoped to see Christians [in office], yet by the Constitution, a papist, or an infidel was as eligible as they." In New Hampshire the fear was of "a papist, a Mohomatan [sic], a deist, yea an atheist at the helm of government." Henry Abbot, a delegate to the North Carolina convention, warned that "the exclusion of religious tests" was "dangerous and impolitic" and that "pagans, deists, and Mahometans [sic] might obtain offices among us." If there is no religious test, he asked, "to whom will they [officeholders] swear support—the ancient pagan gods of Jupiter, Juno, Minerva, or Pluto?"

More specific fears were clearly at work here. The absence of religious tests, it was feared, would open up the national government to control by Jews, Catholics, and Quakers. The Reverend David Caldwell, a Presbyterian minister and delegate in North Carolina, worried that the Constitution now offered an invitation to "Jews and pagans of every kind" to govern us. Major Thomas Lusk, a delegate in Massachusetts, denounced Article 6 of the Constitution and shuddered "at the idea that Roman Catholics, Papists, and Pagans might be introduced into office, and that Popery and the Inquisition may be established in America." A delegate in North Carolina waved a pamphlet that depicted the possibility that the pope of Rome might be elected president. Calming himself down, he warned the delegates that in "the course of four or five hundred years" it was most certain that "Papists may occupy that [presidential] chair." More realistically, it was fear of Quakers, and of their pacifism and antislavery views, that helped fuel the debate. In Charleston, South Carolina, a writer in the *City Gazette* warned on January 3, 1788, that "as there will be no religious test," the Quakers "will have weight, in proportion to their numbers, in the great scale of continental government." An anticonstitutional article written for the *New York Daily Advertiser* that same January and widely reprinted within days in Connecticut, New Hampshire, and Massachusetts papers pulled no punches about the social repercussions of Article 6. No religious tests admitted to national lawmaking: "1st. Quakers, who will make the blacks saucy, and at the same time deprive us of the means of defence—2dly. Mahometans, who ridicule the doctrine of the Trinity—3dly. Deists, abominable wretches—4thly. Negroes, the seed of Cain—5thly. Beggars, who when set on horseback will ride to the devil—6thly. Jews etc. etc." Not quite finished with the last, the newspaper writer feared that since the Constitution stupidly gave command of the whole militia to the president, "should he hereafter be a Jew, our dear posterity may be ordered to rebuild Jerusalem."

The prohibition of religious tests was seen by many opponents as the operative sign of the Constitution's more basic flaw—its general godless quality, its seeming indifference to religion. Disputants around America complained, as the writer "Philadelphiensis" did in November 1787, of the framers' "silence" and "indifference about religion." An anonymous writer in the *Virginia Independent Chronicle* cautioned in October 1787 about "the pernicious effects" of the Constitution's "general disregard of religion," its "cold indifference towards religion." Thomas Wilson, also of Virginia, insisted that the "Constitution is de[i]stical in principle, and in all probability the composers had no thought of God in all their consultations." There is some truth in Mr. Wilson's observation. When Benjamin Franklin, who presided over the Constitutional Convention, urged the delegates to open their sessions with prayers, a request cited often today by the religious right, the delegates, more worried about worldly matters like Shays's Rebellion and America's financial instability under the Articles of Confederation, voted to adjourn for the day rather than discuss Franklin's suggestion. The matter was never brought up again.

Deism was, as we shall see, a powerful force among the intellectuals of the founding generation, even among many of the delegates in Philadelphia. A nondoctrinaire religion, deism rejected a supernatural faith built around an anthropomorphic God who intervened in human affairs, either in answer to prayer or for other, inscrutable reasons. Instead, it posited a naturalistic religion with a God understood as a supreme intelligence who after creating the world destined it to operate forever after according to natural, rational, and scientific laws. No surprise, then, that a frequent claim heard in 1787 and 1788 was that the Constitution represented a deistic conspiracy to overthrow the Christian commonwealth. This view was most powerfully put by the Carlisle, Pennsylvania, pamphleteer "Aristocrotis" in a piece aptly titled "The Government of Nature Delineated or An Exact Picture of the New Federal Constitution."

Aristocrotis contends that the delegates in Philadelphia have created a government that for the first time in world history removes religion from public life. Until 1787 "there was never a nation in the world whose government was not circumscribed by religion." But this was no problem for the Constitutional Convention intent on creating "a government founded upon nature." What, he asks, "is the world to the federal convention but as the drop of a bucket, or the small dust in the balance! What the world could not accomplish from the commencement of time till now, they easily performed in a few moments by declaring that 'no religious test shall ever be required as a qualification to any office, or public trust, under the United States.' " This, Aristocrotis suggests, "is laying the ax to the root of the tree; whereas other nations only lopped off a few noxious branches." He argues that the "new Constitution, disdains . . . belief of a deity, the immortality of the soul, or the resurrection of the body, a day of judgement, or a future state of rewards and punishments," because its authors are committed to a natural religion that is deistic nonreligion. He concludes with irony: "If some religion must be had the religion of nature will certainly be preferred by a government founded upon the law of nature. One great argument in favor of this religion is, that most of the members of the grand convention are great admirers of it; and they certainly are the best models to form our religious as well as our civil belief on."

Other critics of the Constitution shared Aristocrotis' demand for the retention of a Christian commonwealth, with a similar desire to see religion be an integral part of public life. In New Hampshire, "A Friend to the Rights of the People," writing against "the discarding of all religious tests," asked in an interesting shift, "Will this be good policy to discard all religion?" The answer was, of course, no, for despite the Constitution "it is acknowledged by all that civil government can't well be supported without the assistance of religion." No man, he concluded, "is fit to be a ruler of protestants, without he can honestly profess to be of the protestant religion." During this same New Hampshire ratification debate, a delegate argued that to ratify the Constitution would be to overturn all religion and introduce a godless America, suggesting even that if the Constitution were adopted "congress might deprive the people of the use of the holy scriptures." An Anti-Federalist writer warned in a Boston newspaper on January 10, 1788, that since God was absent from the Constitution, Americans would suffer the fate that the prophet Samuel foretold to Saul: "because thou hast rejected the word of the Lord, he hath also rejected thee." In short, if Americans in their new fundamental law forgot God and His Christian commonwealth, God would soon forget them, and they would perish. The same apocalyptic theme was picked up by the Massachusetts Anti-Federalist Charles Turner, who feared that "without the presence of Christian piety and morals the best Republican Constitution can never save us from slavery and ruin."

One of the most moving rejections of the godless Constitution in favor of an overtly Christian government came from one "David" in the *Massachusetts Gazette* on March 7, 1788. His message was clear. Public virtue and civic peace required governmental encouragement of and involvement with Christian religion. He defended Massachusetts' "religious test, which requires all public officers to be of some Christian, protestant persuasion," and criticized the federal Constitution's "public inattention" to religion and the framers' "leaving religion to shift wholly for itself." The new nation was embarking on a futile course, for "it is more difficult to build an elegant house without tools to work with, than it is to establish a durable government without the publick protection of religion."

A letter to the delegates at the Virginia ratifying convention in June 1788 urged them to insist on adding to the first or second article of the Constitution a clause requiring the creation "at every proper place through the United States" of academies regulated by Congress where young people would learn "the principles of the Christian religion without regard to any sect, but pure and unadulterated as left by its divine author and his apostle." The social benefits expected to flow from these obligatory Christian academies sound very much like a 1788 version of the projected fruits of compulsory school prayer as urged by today's Christian right. Were compulsory Christian education established, the Virginian affirms, "we would have fewer law suits, less backbiting, slander, and mean observations, more industry, justice and real happiness than at present."

Like this Virginian, those opposed to the godless Constitution did not just complain; their advocacy of a Christian commonwealth led them to propose specific changes in the Constitution at various state ratifying conventions, all of which were rejected. In Connecticut, William Williams, a delegate, formally moved that the Constitution's one-sentence preamble be enlarged to include a Christian conception of politics. He proposed that it be changed to read, "We the people of the United States in a firm belief of the being and perfection of the one living and true God, the creator and supreme Governor of the World, in His universal providence and the authority of His laws: that He will require of all moral agents an account of their conduct, that all rightful powers among men are ordained of, and mediately derived from God, therefore in a dependence on His blessing and acknowledgment of His efficient protection in establishing our Independence, whereby it is become necessary to agree upon and settle a Constitution of federal government for ourselves, and in order to form a more perfect union, etc., as it is expressed in the present introduction, do ordain, etc." Williams also moved that a religious test along these lines be required for all federal officials. One hundred and sixty years later the Pledge of Allegiance might be changed by Congress to include the brief "under God." But in 1788 the delegates in Connecticut chose not to introduce God, via Williams's wordy resolution, into the U.S. Constitution.

Equally unsuccessful was the Virginia initiative in April and May 1788 to change the wording of Article 6 itself. "No religious test shall ever be required as a qualification to any office of public trust under the United States" became "no *other* religious test shall ever be required *than a* belief in the one only true God, who is the rewarder of the good, and the punisher of the evil." This change was rejected.

The defenders of Article 6 were, of course, equally outspoken. Twice in February 1788, in the *Federalist* Nos. 51 and 56, James Madison cited the "no religious test" clause as one of the glories of the new Constitution. "The door," Madison wrote, "of the Federal Government, is open to merit of every description, whether native or adoptive, whether young or old, and without regard to poverty or wealth, or to any particular profession of religious faith."

Tenche Coxe, a wealthy merchant and former member of the Continental Congress from Philadelphia, thrilled to America's unique and bold departure from the heavy hand of religious meddling in politics. A foremost recommendation of the new Constitution, he wrote in October 1787, is that "no religious test is ever to be required" for the servants of the American people. In Italy, Spain, and Portugal public office was denied to Protestants and "in England, every Presbyterian, and other person not of their established church, is incapable of holding an office." The convention in Philadelphia had then "the honor of proposing the first public act, by which any nation" declared that public service is for "any wise or good citizen." "Danger from ecclesiastical tyranny, that long standing and still remaining curse of the people," Coxe wrote, "can be feared by no man in the United States." He envisioned great economic potential for America as a result of its novel path. The "no religious test" clause constituted, he suggested, a declaration of freedom to all the world, and he predicted that, like Holland, America would become "an asylum of religious liberty," which would produce the same economic vitality and success that graced tolerant Holland.

In North Carolina the critics of the absence of religious tests were pointedly answered by James Iredell, future associate justice of the U.S. Supreme Court. Test laws, he argued, were a vile form of "discrimination." Their ban was a guarantee in the Constitution of the "principle of religious freedom." He had no problem with the possibility that Americans may choose "representatives who have no religion at all, and that pagans and Mahometans" may be elected. How, he asks, "is it possible to exclude any set of men" without thus laying "the foundation on which persecution has been raised in every part of the world." For a New York writer the absence of religious tests signified the Constitution's "relief of the mind from religious thraldom, which has been productive of so many evils in other countries."

The "no religious test" clause also had clerical supporters. The Virginia Baptist leader John Leland lauded Article 6 for its consistency with his conviction that the integrity of religious faith required governmental noninvolvement in religion. Samuel Spencer in North Carolina insisted that religion stand on its own "without any connection with temporal authority." Making a similar argument, indeed calling the absence of religious tests "one of the great ornaments of the Constitution," was the Reverend Samuel Langdon of New Hampshire. He told the New Hampshire ratifying convention that he "took a general view of religion as unconnected with and detached from the civil power—that [as] it was an obligation between God and his creatures, the civil authority could not interfere without infringing upon the rights of conscience."

At the Massachusetts convention a Congregational minister, the Reverend Daniel Shute, argued that religious tests for office deprived citizens of their civil rights. "Who should be excluded from national trusts?" he asked. "Whatever bigotry may suggest, the dictates of candor and equity, I conceive, will be, none," even, he added, "those who have no other guide, in the way to virtue and heaven, than the dictates of natural religion." At the same convention a distinguished Baptist minister, the Reverend Isaac Backus, supported the absence of a religious test. "Nothing is more evident," he commented, "both in reason and The Holy Scriptures, than that religion is ever a matter between God and individuals; and, therefore, no man or men can impose any religious test without invading the essential prerogatives of our Lord Jesus Christ. . . . And let the history of all nations be searched . . . and it will appear that the imposing of religious tests had been the greatest engine of tyranny in the world." So much for religious correctness for the Reverend Backus.

In a wonderfully American coalition, there stood alongside these clerical defenders of Article 6 a number of unabashed advocates of secularism who gloried in the very godlessness of the Constitution. Such was one "Elihu," whose self-proclaimed deistic defense of the Constitution was printed in Connecticut and Massachusetts newspapers in February 1788. The Constitution, he wrote, is a rational document for a wise people in an enlightened age. The time has passed "when nations could be kept in awe with stories of God's sitting with legislators and dictating laws." The exclusion of religious tests was a glorious step, for no longer would politicians and clerics use religion "to establish their own power on the credulity of the people, shackling their uninformed minds with incredible tales." Sounding much like the French Enlightenment writers who, we shall see, so influenced Jefferson, Elihu claimed that the Constitution created a political order appropriate for the new age when "the light of philosophy has arisen . . . miracles have ceased, oracles are silenced, monkish darkness is dissipated. . . . Mankind are no longer to be deluded with fable." The most brilliant achievement of the Constitution's framers, Elihu noted, is that they have refused "to dazzle even the superstitious, by a hint about grace or ghostly knowledge. They come to us in the plain language of common sense, and propose to our understanding a system of government, as the invention of mere human wisdom; no deity comes down to dictate it, not even a god appears in a dream to propose any part of it."

Yet another thinker holding nondogmatic religious beliefs, William Van Murray, Esq., applauded the absence of religious tests in a 1787 essay in the *American Museum*. America, he wrote, "will be the great philosophical theater of the world," since its Constitution recognizes that "Christians are not the only people there." Religious tests are "A VIOLATION of THE LAW OF NATURE." Governments are created, he held, according to the "laws of nature. These are unacquainted with the distinctions of religious opinion; and of the terms Christian, Mohamentan, Jew or Gentile."

Lest Elihu's and Van Murray's enlightened and secular readings of the Constitution appear to be the eccentric rantings of men hostile to religion, we should note the similarity of their arguments to that offered by the more sober, moderate, and famous John Adams. Writing in 1786, just before the federal Constitution was written, he took it as given that political constitutions were wholly secular enterprises free of godly involvement or inspiration. "The United States of America," he wrote, marks "the first example of governments erected on the simple principles of nature." The architects of American governments never "had interviews with the gods or were in any degree under the inspiration of Heaven." Government, Adams insisted, is "contrived merely by the use of reason and the senses." Adams's view of constitution making is also caught up in the secular ideals of the Age of Reason. "Neither the people nor their conventions, committees, or subcommittees," he wrote, "considered legislation in any other light than as ordinary arts and sciences, only more important. . . . The people were universally too enlightened to be imposed on by artifice. . . . [G]overnments thus founded on the natural authority of the people alone, without a pretense of miracle or mystery, and which are destined to spread over the northern part of that whole quarter of the globe, are a great point gained in favour of the rights of mankind."

In the fierce debate over the "no religious test" clause itself, Adams's secular view of politics is best found in the lengthy defense of Article 6 published under the name "A Landholder" on

December 17, 1787, for the *Connecticut Courant* and widely reprinted in nearby states. The author was no ordinary Connecticut farmer, however; he was Oliver Ellsworth, recently a delegate to the federal Constitutional Convention in Philadelphia, who would soon be a member of the first U.S. Congress and eventually, for a brief time, chief justice of the U.S. Supreme Court. Seeking to persuade the Connecticut ratifying convention to approve the Constitution, Ellsworth provides a veritable lecture on the relationship of religion and politics, especially of "systems of religious error adopted in times of ignorance." He excoriates the English Test Acts (whose story will be told in a later chapter) for seeking to exclude first Catholics and then Protestant dissenters from the political realm. From his detailed account of these acts, he suggests, "there arises an unfavorable presumption against them." Even more significant, "they are useless, tyrannical, and peculiarly unfit for the people of this country."

A religious test would be absurd in America, Ellsworth argues; there are too many denominations. To favor one religious sect with public office would incapacitate the many others "and thus degrade them from the rank of freemen." What, then, of a general test, reserving public office to those who proclaim the simple belief in God and the divine authority of the Scriptures? Ellsworth rejects this as well, for an unprincipled man could easily dissemble and proclaim such beliefs simply to qualify for public office. At this point, Ellsworth moves from his practical arguments against religious tests to his main theoretical concern:

> To come to the true principle. . . . The business of civil government is to protect the citizen in his rights. . . . civil government has no business to meddle with the private opinions of the people. . . . I am accountable not to man, but to God, for the religious opinions which I embrace. . . . A test law is . . . the offspring of error and the spirit of persecution. Legislatures have no right to set up an inquisition and examine into the private opinions of men.

Arguments like Ellsworth's proved successful in keeping the U.S. Constitution godless in the state ratification votes of 1787 and 1789, as they would be in the nineteenth century, as we shall note below, in rebuffing the periodic efforts to rewrite the Constitution's preamble to include a definitive commitment to the Christian religion. But what about those states' own constitutions, many of which required officeholders to be Protestants or believers in a Christian God? The reactions varied, with some states preserving the older view that good rulers had to believe in God. The Pennsylvania constitution dropped its religious test in 1790, insisting only that officeholders be supporters of the Constitution. In 1792 Delaware added to its constitution a "no religious test" clause. Georgia and South Carolina followed quickly. But Vermont and New Jersey retained their religious tests for officeholders until 1844, and New Hampshire its until 1877. New states entering the Union in the nineteenth century occasionally did include in their constitutions the requirement that officeholders believe in the Christian God. Not until 1961, in fact, did all state constitutional religious tests fall, with the Supreme Court's ruling in *Torasco* v. *Watkins* that the Maryland constitution could not require, as it did (though no longer enforced), that state officers be Christians.

Among those who shared this secular ideal of excluding religion from politics were some, it should be noted, who worried that the existence of the "no religious test" clause might actually imply that politics would, in turn, not be excluded from religion. A wall of separation, after all, prevents trespassing in both directions. Paradoxically, then, some opposed Article 6 because it suggested to them that the Constitution did not go far enough in creating a state utterly uninterested in religion. An opponent of the Constitution, for example, wrote in the *New York Journal* in November 1787 that it left the liberty of conscience unprotected. The prohibition of religious tests, he argued, implies that the new American state could in general regulate religion and matters of private conscience, but specifically denies itself this one power to impose religious tests. Similarly, Governor Edmund Randolph, a supporter of the Constitution, wrote to Madison in February 1788 that he heard some ask, "Does not the exception as to a religious test imply, that the Congress by the general words had power over religion?"

Such critics of Article 6 were, of course, offering friendly amendments to the godless Constitution, literally so. They were part of the larger chorus that during the ratification process insisted that a truly secular state required even more, a specific provision in the document that protects the private rights of conscience. The laissez-faire liberal American state leaving individuals alone with their own religious beliefs evolves next and almost immediately with the First Amendment, championed by those outspoken theorists of the secular state—Madison and Jefferson. We must, however, acknowledge here, as the writer in the *Virginia Independent Chronicle* did in October 1787, that the U.S. Constitution is "coldly indifferent towards religion," and a good thing too.

There remains a crucial final reminder. The political convictions of the men who struggled to ratify a godless Constitution were not products of personal godlessness. Far from it. Almost everyone who participated in the debates about the Constitution shared a concern about the health of religion. The success of democracy depended upon a moral citizenry; and for most American thinkers of the eighteenth century, morality rested on some sort of religious convictions. So did a theory of human rights. Many of the men who championed the godless Constitution stayed aloof from dogmatic forms of Christian faith, but most of them believed in a God who rewarded good and punished evil in an afterlife. They respected the moral teachings of Christ and hoped that they would prosper among Americans and in the churches that Americans attended. So why did they refuse to assign government, whose very existence depended upon morality, any responsibility for promoting religion?

The answer to that question follows in the next three chapters and pushes us back in time to English thinkers of the seventeenth century and to the experience of the American colonists with the mother country and with their own colonial governments. What we shall also discover is that while the idea of a godless constitution clearly incorporated certain secular ideals, important and forceful justifications for such a secular document lay in religious thought. No one in American experience has cared more about religion than Roger Williams. And virtually no one in American experience has fashioned a stronger argument for a godless politics. We turn first to his story.

CHAPTER THREE

ROGER WILLIAMS AND THE RELIGIOUS ARGUMENT FOR CHURCH-STATE SEPARATION

ROGER WILLIAMS WAS ahead of his time. An ardent Puritan, described by John Winthrop as a "godly minister," Williams arrived in the Massachusetts Bay Colony in 1631, only one year after the disembarkation of the first sizable group of settlers. As the articulate and well-loved minister of the church in Salem, he was a prominent citizen. However, almost immediately he started to complain about the ways of New England, complaints that the magistrates of Massachusetts Bay regarded as "dangerous opinions." Williams challenged the legality of the charter the Massachusetts Bay leaders had secured from Charles I. He argued that the settlers ought to declare formally that they had separated from the inadequately reformed Church of England. He denied that their efforts to create a Godly commonwealth made them special favorites of divine providence. Most of all he criticized Massachusetts Bay for its religious intolerance.

In order to appreciate the shock waves caused by that last complaint of Williams, we must remember that the first English colonists who came to North America had no intention of establishing religious freedom, in the sense that we understand the concept. Most English colonists throughout the seventeenth century and for much of the eighteenth little valued the sort of religious toleration that most of us now take for granted. Rather, they were heirs to the ideal of the Christian commonwealth, an ideal as old as the New Testament and as current as the agenda of today's Christian right. Its central assumption is the fusion of religion and politics as proclaimed in Romans 13: "The powers that be are ordained by God," which itself built upon the exhortation of the prophet Isaiah that magistrates had to be like "Nursing Fathers" in the task God had given them to protect and promote religion and, thus, public morality.

The voices of American Indians, African slaves, European Catholics, and English Quakers tell us that the Christian commonwealths established in the colonies were not tolerant places. But so do the words of the Protestant colonists who were determined to use the power of the state to enforce religious orthodoxy. They were not ashamed of their opinions and of the reasons why they did not believe in free religious practice of the sort we profess. Hypocrisy was not their problem, but ours. When they spoke of religious liberty, they meant the liberty to practice religion as they saw fit and to penalize anyone who disagreed with them. When Americans began to talk about religious freedom in its modern sense, as they did when they ratified the "no religious test" clause and when they adopted the First Amendment to the American Constitution, they were reacting not to the tyranny of Old England but to restrictive practices they had experienced at their own hands. When Williams challenged those restrictions, he was practically all alone.

As a result, the magistrates of Massachusetts Bay in 1636 banished Williams, and he went off to found his own colony of Rhode Island along the shores of Narragansett Bay. Williams got into trouble principally because he was determined to secularize the institutions of government and politics in ways that baffled and disturbed his Puritan contemporaries. Yet the interesting thing about his case is that he shared most of the religious convictions of his fellow New England colonists who shipped him off into the wilderness. What distinguished Williams from the rest was the strictness of his religious opinions, his refusal to compromise, his fanaticism, if you like. When he wrote *The Bloudy Tenent of Persecution* in 1644, which is a pioneering document proposing church-state separation, and in his subsequent writings that sought to free churches from the designs of political men and to denounce a Christianity that tried to set the political agenda for civil magistrates, Williams pursued more rigorously than any other person of his day the implications for politics of the Calvinist doctrine of human sin.

To praise Williams is not to denigrate John Winthrop and other admirable seventeenth-century Puritan leaders of the Massachusetts Bay Colony. But it is to remember why in 1787 Americans chose to model their views more on the church-state ideas of Williams than on those of the people who banished him to Rhode Island. The underpinning of his radical views was strictly religious. Because Williams believed that his Christian God had fixed a narrow path of religious duty for his chosen saints, a duty that required them to protect correct Christian practice from worldly corruption, and because he further believed that the number of true Christians would always be a small proportion of the population in any society, he rejected the concept of a nation under God. For England or for Massachusetts Bay to make a claim that it was a Christian polity, a civil government party to a divine contract, was arrogant blasphemy.

To be sure, seventeenth-century American colonists, who in most cases supported a church establishment, took some significant steps, without any influence from Williams, to move church and state apart. In the southern colonies, where the Church of

England maintained its full prerogatives as a national church and where everyone born into the realm was assumed to be a member, that initiative was not so much a matter of principle as a matter of lax practice and the complete absence of bishops and archbishops of the church. The clerics of the Anglican establishment preferred a comfortable life in fair England to the dismal circumstances that made daily life in the Virginia colony a severe trial.

In the New England colonies of Massachusetts Bay and Connecticut, certain aspects of church-state separation were more carefully considered. Everything in these Puritan colonies was carefully considered. Puritans had won their name because they were not satisfied that the English church had totally cleansed itself of Catholic impurities. The formal political power that was given to archbishops in England and the political patronage that tied priests to the state were to them aspects of lingering error. Therefore, by design in Massachusetts Bay, ministers held no political offices. No ecclesiastical courts existed. Church officials gained their titles from elections held by church members, not by a sacred investiture whose sanction ran finally to the crown.

From our perspective, however, colonial New England still looks like a theocracy, and for good reason. The churches of Massachusetts Bay and Connecticut were established churches. That is, the residents of the colonies were taxed to pay for their upkeep and for the salaries of ministers. It did not matter whether they were members of a church or not. It did not matter whether they wanted to be members of some other kind of church, for during the first decades of settlement no other church was allowed. Only male church members could vote in civil elections, and the law required everyone to attend the local church chartered by the civil government. Ministers might not hold civil office, but they delivered sermons on election days and frequently consulted with civil magistrates. The first Puritan citizens of New England committed themselves collectively to do what they believed God, their God, wanted them to do. They did not delude themselves into thinking that everybody in Massachusetts Bay was a sincere Christian. But they did expect all citizens to behave like sincere Christians and not to say anything contrary to Christian belief or to the established Christian practices of the colony.

The men and women who boarded the *Arbella* in 1630 with John Winthrop, leaving England for Massachusetts Bay, believed that they were repeating the biblical drama of Exodus. Following dictates laid down in a covenant with God, they were fleeing, figuratively speaking, from Egypt to Canaan. Their religious leaders taught them that if they obeyed God's word, the nation would prosper. If they fell into the sordid habits of Babylon, God would invent instruments of national retribution. John Winthrop put the matter most famously aboard the *Arbella:* God "hath taken us to be His after a most strickt and peculiar manner . . . wee are entered into Covenant with Him for this worke, wee have taken out a Commission. . . . Now if the Lord shall please to heare us, and bring us in peace to the place wee desire, then hath hee ratified this Covenant and sealed our Commission, [and] will expect a strickt performance of the Articles contained in it. . . ." With these words Winthrop gave the American Puritans their duty to construct a city on a hill. While this duty was both civil and religious, its ultimate success depended upon the power of the civil authorities to enforce religious correctness. Since the authority of ministers did not extend beyond their individual church, following the system of religious organization we call congregationalism, religious orthodoxy depended upon the political men who ruled the colony.

For Roger Williams, this situation was as bad as what had existed in Christendom before the Reformation. He began his argument to change the political practices of his fellow New England Puritans by rejecting their use of the Exodus story. By his reckoning, the special relation that God had with ancient Israel, a relation broken at the beginning of the Jewish diaspora, had not been renewed later with any other nation. No modern nation performed any special work of God. New England was not a redeemed Israel. A howling wilderness, yes, but not one that led to Canaan. Massachusetts Bay was not a Christian state, for there was no such thing. European monarchs who referred to their nation as part of Christendom lied. They ruled over societies filled with sinners and hypocrites. In Williams's mind, being a Christian entailed something more than fulfilling one's civic duties. Civic duties were important, but they had nothing to do with Christian salvation and God's plans for eternity. "In respect of the Lord's special property to one country more than another," Williams wrote, "what difference between Asia and Africa, between Europe and America, between England and Turkey, London and Constantinople."

New England's treatment of Roger Williams, its almost simultaneous banishment of Anne Hutchinson for relying on her inner light to know God's will rather than on the words of the magistrates, the later execution of Quakers and witches—these were acts of religious intolerance common under seventeenth-century Christian governments. We are bound, all the same, to acknowledge that much about these old Puritan regimes in New England was admirable. Non-Puritans who traveled there hoping to march to different religious drummers had fair warning of their unfriendly reception. "Love it or leave it" is a fair rendering of the social motto. As societies go, Puritanism in New England provided a framework for a peaceable kingdom. Without armies or police, it made freely chosen patterns of moral behavior the basis of social order. The success of the social order in Massachusetts Bay and Connecticut undoubtedly owed many debts to the collective belief in a divine covenant. Their leaders, in refusing to see value in religious pluralism or any other sort of heterogeneity, cited a divine mandate. If many people in our own day seem to be unduly nostalgic for a society dedicated to Christian uniformity, the example of New England in the early seventeenth century helps explain their longing.

People attacked Williams as a radical, a "church-ruinating" anarchist, for laying the ideological foundation for a society that takes religion seriously but constructs a state without reference to any religious claims. Such a society is not secular, if by that we mean that religion plays no role in public life. Its politics, however, is godless, and so, in their official functions, are its politicians. Williams reached his conclusions about the urgent need to separate church and state, not because he did not care about the future of Christianity, but because he sometimes appeared to care about nothing else. Williams's main concern was always the purity of the church.

Born in 1603, Williams, like many other English Protestants, became absorbed in millennial predictions. Christ would come again to effect a final purification of his church. Nothing was more important for Christians than working to prepare for that final act of history. Although, literally speaking, Christian men and women could do nothing to assist God, they were obligated to at least watch for the signs of God's impending judgments, separate themselves from the temptations of the world, and prepare their hearts. When Williams studied at Cambridge, he still entertained the hope that England, under the direction of the monarch, would be the site of God's redemptive drama. But he changed his views. Williams grew absolutely convinced that God favored no nation over another and that civil governments had no role to play in the millennial drama. Nothing in the Book of Revelation foretold a glorious mediating role for any civil state. The earnest Christians' efforts to cleanse the church, a quest that troubled Williams for the rest of his life, sought no assistance from the state. Religious purity and good government were two separate issues.

Williams's religious questing led him in some eccentric directions. Finally, he questioned the spiritual authority of all organized
churches. However, the strictly theological aspects of his later
thought need not concern us. If Williams had interested himself
only with religion, he would not figure in our story. He did, in
fact, give his attention to secular matters. After he went off to
Rhode Island, he found himself saddled with many proprietary
and political duties, including the need to secure a charter for his
colony, which he finally managed to do in 1644, over considerable opposition in England. He recognized commercial possibilities for Rhode Island. He moreover served as president, the chief
civil magistrate of the colony, for three years beginning in 1654,
and was a leading figure in Rhode Island's not always successful
negotiations with local Indian tribes. The question how this
deeply religious man combined his sense of religious mission with
his civic responsibilities lies at the center of his importance to
American history.

Specifically, we can interrogate Williams the state builder on
three crucial issues. First, should civil magistrates necessarily be
godly men or religious believers? Second, if it is granted that the
state should not support churches financially, should government
in other direct or indirect ways promote religion? Third, is religious belief ever relevant to public policy? Williams's answer to
the first two questions was no. His answer to the third was complicated. Let us examine those answers closely and consider
Williams's views about the consequences that flowed from his answers. We will have little trouble making what Williams said in
response to his critics relevant to contemporary debate.

On the importance of distinguishing the skills of governors
from their religious profession, Williams was explicit: "We know
the many excellent gifts wherewith it hath pleased God to furnish
many, inabling them for publike service to their Countries both
in peace and war (as all ages and experience testifies) on whose

soules hee hath not yet pleased to shine in the face of Jesus Christ." To be a Christian was not a worldly skill. A person could farm successfully and not be a Christian. A woman could spin and cook in an extraordinary way and not be a Christian. People could love one another and take care of their children and not be Christians. The common ways of the world went forward with or without Christian ministrations. History provided many examples of wise rulers who were not Christian and who provided no special favors to people who claimed to be Christian. "A pagan or anti-Christian pilot may be as skillful to carry the ship to its desired port as any Christian mariner or pilot in the world and may perform that work with as much safety and speed." Protestants, Williams thought, should never forget how badly things had gone for both church and state when civil rulers had felt beholden to "lie down and creep" before the pope's outstretched ring.

Government was a human creation, "merely human and civil," one of the unfortunate conditions imposed upon humankind by the fall. It was absolutely necessary because some authority had to preserve people in their persons and property. It could be good or bad. But Williams did not view government as redemptive. Government did not exist to smooth the route of its citizens toward eternal salvation. When it absurdly took upon itself the task of making people holy and acceptable to God, it only produced monumental hypocrisy among both the rulers and the ruled. Government existed because God did *not* rule the world.

Williams never imagined that governing was an easy task. He simply said that it wasn't a specifically Christian or religious task. The political skills necessary to preserve civil peace might as easily be found among Jews, or Turks, or Chinese as among people who professed Christianity. Sound government existed in "nations, cities, kingdoms . . . which never heard of the true God, nor His holy son." True, in Rhode Island in the seventeenth century, people who claimed to be Christians were more likely to become magistrates of the colony than infidels were. That fact, however, had no necessary implications for better government. Williams wanted no religious test for public office in Rhode Island. No one in civil government, he thought, should swear an oath before God. The measures of a good ruler simply were not the measures of a good Christian.

On empirical grounds, Williams had an excellent case, however much his conclusion was denounced by other godly men in Old and New England. The political foundations of modern Western states lie in ancient Greece and Rome. Every textbook on the history of Western civilization asks students to respect the political genius of Nebuchadnezzar, of Hammurabi, of Solon, of Pericles, of Julius Caesar, of Augustus Caesar. Not one of them was Christian. Not one of them even stood within the tradition of religious monotheism. Many of them certainly mixed religion and politics, but that is not usually held these days to be the reason for their success. When Williams was conducting his own experiments in good government, he knew that effective governments existed in many places where there were no Christians. He also knew that many professing Christians made bad rulers. To prove that point to himself, he had only to look at the despised Antichrist who headed the Roman Catholic Church. England, too, furnished examples of good monarchs and bad monarchs whose success or failure had nothing to do with piety or its lack. It might even be that good rulers had to do things that good Christians ought not to do.

What remains radical about Williams's views even today is not just that his notion of "no religious test" meant a Jew might rule over a society where most people are nominal Christians. Even Jerry Falwell has swallowed hard and gone along with that. It is that Williams also included nonbelievers, nontheists, in the category of people who might rule well. As it happened, no atheists presented themselves for public office in colonial Rhode Island.

That should not surprise us. What might surprise us, however, given that atheism or nontheism is far more common in the twentieth century, is that they don't often present themselves for public office now. To declare oneself a nontheist is de facto to disqualify oneself for the office of president of the United States. One's religion is more of an issue in this country of religious disestablishment than in most countries where religious establishment still exists.

This is to say that a large portion of the American electorate thinks, contrary to Williams, that a good ruler must believe in God. We have powerful evidence that this is not true. We also have powerful evidence that many people who believe in God are not especially virtuous. In fact, our informal test that forces office seekers to mouth religious platitudes leads more often than not, as Williams predicted, to shameless pandering by politicians and what is quite literally an exploitation of God. Perhaps the de facto religious test for political office results from Americans' long-standing fear of government and their altogether correct notion that democratic politics, being an eminently corruptible business, needs all the help from normative morals that it can get. For many people, a formulaic recitation of religious oaths is necessary in public life. Yet perhaps this requirement only means that we do not take either religion or government seriously enough. We are trying to make the one perform the business of the other.

Williams's position with respect to our second posed question flows from the logic of his position on the first. If civil magistrates may perform their functions irrespective of the state of their eternal souls, then they certainly have no role to perform in the creation or the custody of the purified church. That task belongs to God's scattered saints. Even if the civil magistrates in colonial New England were by chance men who stood among God's elect, and Williams would have cautiously accorded that distinction to himself as well as to his old rival John Winthrop, they were not in their civil capacity charged to advance the cause of true religion. Nor did Williams accept the argument that they should promote religion because piety was an essential component of good citizenship.

The only way that civil magistrates could promote religion was to pay no attention to it at all. There were several arguments for this novel proposition. In simplest terms, government was the business of men, and the church was the business of God. For a magistrate to presume to protect true religion was to usurp the place of God. Williams also saw a practical danger in confusing the two roles. Civil magistrates could not be trusted with religious duties. Whenever civil rulers had emerged as would-be protectors or champions of religion, they had appropriated religion to profane interests—to their own quest for profit and power. Nations, for example, often went to war. Governments in fact had legitimate reasons to go to war. One of those reasons, however, was not to help God redeem humankind. Here Williams again drew a contrast between ancient Israel and the nations of his own day. Whenever a contemporary ruler arose to protect true religion by the sword, he did true religion an incalculable harm. The only weapons to advance religion were spiritual ones, and civil magistrates did not wield them.

Williams, we must not forget, cared passionately about true religion. However, since he came to believe that no organized church possessed all of God's truth, he concluded that any effort to sanction by law an official religion impeded the advance of God's millennial church. In one sense Williams was not at all tolerant. He believed that some religious positions—his own, for example—contained more truth than others. Most religions contained errors that in Williams's opinion consigned their adherents to eternal damnation. For that reason, his justification of tolerance may strike us as lacking in exuberance. He did not allow Jews and Catholics into Rhode Island because he respected their religious opinions or because he attached positive value to religious pluralism. For Quakers, Williams held as much contempt as any of the leaders of Massachusetts Bay who had steadily persecuted them. They were guilty of "high treason against the King of Kings." For Williams, to tolerate did not mean to renounce attacks. He relentlessly subjected the ideas and practices of Quakers to public ridicule. People might be free in Rhode Island to persist in their religious error, but that did not mean that they would not be reminded of it.

However, they would not be reminded of it by the state. Williams's assault upon Quakers was in his mind neither a political act nor an act that had political significance. If Quakers were unfit for public office, it was not because of their religious consciences but because their religious beliefs, pacifism in particular, made them poor governors. In no case was it government's function to encourage or discourage any religious practice, particularly in any way that might seem to place a government stamp of approval upon one sort of religious practice as opposed to another.

In Williams's mind it was clear what government should not do. It should not declare an official church or a state religion. It should not tax people to pay the salaries of ministers or to build church buildings, even if such tax money were divided in some equitable way among all religious groups. It should not compel people to go to church. It should not make blasphemy a crime or enforce as part of civil law the first table of the Ten Commandments. Those first four of the Exodus commandments prescribed the obligation of Jews and Christians to God and had no bearing on the civil state. Williams would not have permitted government to write Sunday blue laws. He would not have countenanced laws that banned certain artistic representations as irreligious. He would not have put people in jail for swearing, unless the swearing stemmed from belligerent behavior that threatened public peace.

It is interesting to speculate what Williams would have said about prayer in public schools, about whether churches should be tax exempt, or about whether churches that were tax exempt could practice racial or gender discrimination in choosing their members and leaders. It may also be an exercise in distortion, for even recognizing that Williams was a man of unusual consistency, we must allow for the fact that principled people change their minds when they confront new circumstances. Today government and organized religions do many things that they did not do in the seventeenth century. Churches then did not build hospitals or own fishing fleets. Government then did not provide church-founded universities with money to carry on scientific research. One thing is certain. Williams would not have regarded the institutional health of many organized religions in the United States as a sign of spiritual purity or of progress toward the millennium. If New England was not in his mind a Christian society in the seventeenth century, America in the late twentieth century is by the high standards of Roger Williams most certainly not a Christian nation.

This last observation may at least suggest how Williams would regard elected officials who make it their duty to find a way for children to pray in public schools. That ambition, even if it is not guided by a desire to curry favor with voters and to avoid a host of difficult issues more relevant to their responsibilities as public officials, would constitute in Williams's mind an effort by government to prescribe what was proper religious practice. As such, it ought to be resisted by any religious group that takes its own practices seriously. He would also regard it as an effort to draw a divine sanction over something that is not sacred. In repudiating the issue of prayer as inappropriate for a political or social agenda, Williams would have accepted the general proposition that religion is private. As always, Williams considered the good of religion before the good of the state. The state cannot touch a religious practice without corrupting it.

If only everything could be kept so clear. However, the real difficulty begins with the third question raised by Williams's thought. In any practical situation this question bears on the first two: Is religious belief ever relevant to public policy? In any society where religion is important and where a large number of people take it with great seriousness as a base of social morality, religion can never be private, in the sense of irrelevant to public issues. Williams lived in a society where religion mattered, and he took religion seriously. He might argue, as he did, that religious leaders had no business telling civil magistrates what to do, just as he forbade the magistrates to intrude into church affairs. But that formula, though it settled much, did not settle everything. In the first place, Williams himself linked religion to morals, and he expected magistrates in Rhode Island to enforce the second table of the Ten Commandments—the commandments that forbade killing, stealing, adultery.

An equally significant issue stems from the way religion may affect the general tone of public life and the expectations people have of their political leaders. Suppose someone had declared publicly in Rhode Island that Christ was a bastard and Mary an adulteress. If Williams had been consistent, he would not have held such a person guilty of a civil crime. But could he possibly have imagined that such a person would make a good governor of the colony? In this case, we must consider a man who has made his religious views relevant to the political process by saying something offensive to most voters. We can easily predict his defeat if he runs for office. That would be as true today as it was in the past. Must we admit, then, that in a society where over 90 percent of the people tell Gallup pollsters that they believe in God, a religious test will inevitably slip in through the back door?

Or can we dismiss our example as merely a case of a dumb politician?

The value of Williams's views is that they force us to think. Clearly we approve of Williams's prescription for a godless politics. Yet even his strict formulations permit ambiguity. In a society where a lot of people share the same general religious beliefs, their cultural biases will alone work to shape public life. Elected officials will not be immune to their influence, not simply because their reelection depends upon it, but because they belong to a community whose many members believe that their shared moral values are rooted in their shared religious beliefs. The difficulty lies in specifying criteria that tell us when the religious biases of voters become an illegitimate injection of God into politics. For Williams such an injection was blasphemy. For many Americans of the present day it runs against the spirit of the Constitution. Yet because people obviously have different opinions about what constitutes illegitimacy in these cases, we have no consensus about criteria. The problem produces the grayest area of church-state separation.

The key point to Williams was always to remember that no society, no government, no nation, played a role in God's redemptive scheme. Religion might influence how people behaved in all areas of their lives. But what they did in the name of God had no claims upon their neighbor's conscience. Elected officials should try in their own way to be virtuous, but they should never claim that they acted in God's name. Williams thought that if everyone understood these fundamentals, the problems of keeping church and state separate would take care of themselves.

His ideas, of course, did not prevent many Protestant leaders in America who lived long after him from persisting in the habit, begun at the founding of Massachusetts Bay, of calling America a redeemer nation. It was a redeemer nation because it was a Christian nation upon which God had showered great blessings.

Look almost anywhere in Protestant church life in the nineteenth century, and the claim is there. The Reverend Josiah Strong, speaking for the American Home Missionary Society in 1885, had no hesitation in "affirming that the signs of divine decree point to this land of ours as the one which is fast gathering to it-self the races which must take the lead in the final conflicts of Christianity for the possession of the world. Ours is the elect na-tion for the age to come. We are the chosen people."

For Williams, however, millennial hope was not politics. If anything was godly about the seventeenth-century society of Rhode Island, that godliness had to do not with what the civil state did but with what it didn't do. The civil state did not try to force people to believe what they could not believe. It did not equate the worthiness of people to perform useful and decent work in the world with their religious beliefs. It did not confuse its suc-cesses with the work of God. Most of all, it did not turn any no-tion of providential favor into a patriotic cry, thereby conflating religion and nationalism. Naming a town Providence had religious overtones. However, any redemptive mission in Rhode Island in the seventeenth century was being accomplished by small bands of God's chosen saints who had separated themselves from the world and who viewed the power of mighty nations as a human rather than a divine creation.

We are still fighting about the implications of Williams's efforts to invent a godless politics. Christians who argued that the state had a duty to enforce religious uniformity, and in the seventeenth century that meant virtually all except Baptists, saw the issue as one of civil peace. Isn't that still true? By this logic, state-spon-sored religious correctness is not an inquisitional effort to ferret out heretics. It is about the duty of the state to preserve good order and decency. The General Court of Massachusetts Bay did not banish Roger Williams for his religious opinions. Not exactly. In the strictest sense, the magistrates executed the civil penalty of banishment against Williams because he threatened the social harmony of the colony.

Williams still saw his case as one of religious persecution, as most of us do as well. However, the effort to link religious correctness with civil peace continues to be part of our present debates. In fact, Williams's religious opinions did bear on civil questions. His accusation that the civil magistrates of Massachusetts Bay blasphemously tried to uphold a divine contract undermined the colony's legal system. His insistence that the churches in the colony separate from the Church of England was linked to his beliefs that the charter Massachusetts Bay had received from the English crown was illegitimate and that the settlers had no right to the land they had usurped from the Indians. The leaders of Massachusetts Bay feared that if they gave up their pretense of being a Christian nation with the power to coerce everyone, whether a genuine Christian or not, into correct Christian behavior, God would punish them. What Williams advanced in the name of religious freedom would have demolished their political system.

Therefore, the quickest way to attack Roger Williams, even after he had founded Rhode Island, was to argue that his ideas produced social disorder. His "pernicious, God-provoking, truth-defacing, church-ruinating, and state-shaking toleration," it was claimed, turned Rhode Island into a sewer of drunkards, debtors, anarchists, and sexual profligates. Sectarian equaled blasphemer equaled lawbreaker. On the one hand, these charges were merely ridiculous. The largest group of religious dissenters in Rhode Island were the Baptists, whose main deviation from the orthodox way of the Massachusetts Bay churches lay in their refusal to practice infant baptism. Like Roger Williams, they were anything but loose in their religious views. They simply carried Puritanism and the principles of church autonomy to extremes. On the other hand, Rhode Island was not in its early years an especially peaceful place, certainly not when compared to Massachusetts Bay. Who can deny that religious uniformity is an effective way to tie a community together? Those of us who champion Roger Williams, the radical, should concede that religious toleration, and the pluralism it produces, often carries with it troublesome social disharmony.

Thus, striking analogies appear between the charges levied against the champions of religious toleration in Rhode Island and the charges levied in our own times against the almost mythical "secular humanist." No one who cares about civil peace would deny that morality is important. In that sense none of the present disputants in American politics argue that moral questions never impinge on public policy issues. The dispute is rather between those who argue that the content of morality is itself a question for public debate and those who argue that morality is an issue already settled by the religious views of a purported majority. To the latter, if public officials don't profess religion, if they don't make a link between proper citizenship and churchgoing, if they don't see to it that schoolchildren pray, then the country is on its way to hell.

The former answer the fear of social disorder with the radical arguments of Roger Williams, who turned the old assumptions upside down. A civil state run by men and women cannot reproduce the kingdom of God that existed at the beginning and would exist again at the end of history. If God had wanted human beings in Eden, He would have left them there. In the world of human beings, religious toleration and the elimination of God-based claims from the civil state have a better chance of producing civil peace than do coercive measures aimed at religious conscience. Religious inquisitions, Williams said, simply put towns "in an uproar." "False and idolatrous practices" do not disturb the civil peace. What does is the "preposterous way" of suppressing and seeking to convert the heretic "by weapons of wrath and blood." Massachusetts Bay achieved social harmony by excluding people who did not agree with its ways. Williams was wise enough to see that that solution in the long run carried more costs than benefits.

In the end Williams believed that secular and sinful men could best rule if they listened to one another rather than dividing themselves into parties based on different views of what God wanted. Even in religious matters there was no certainty. Williams counseled his fellow religious seekers "in these wonderful, searching, disputing, and dissenting times, to search, to listen, to pray, to fast, and more fearfully, more tremblingly to inquire what the holy pleasure and the holy mysteries of the Most Holy are." Of our famous politicians, perhaps only Abraham Lincoln managed to take the religious ideas of Roger Williams and turn them into a vision that countenanced strong political leadership that was deeply moral and religiously informed without linking America's national destiny to the platforms of tinhorn politicians who presumed to act for God. Lincoln had no use for organized religion and ministers who claimed to know what God wanted them to do. During the bloodbath that was America's Civil War, Lincoln puzzled over the fact that both sides prayed to the same God, read the same Bible, and claimed to do His will. Lincoln suspected that if God wanted anything, it was that the leaders who were entrusted to manage a fragile, precious experiment in democratic government remember that what is most assured about humankind is its collective and individual moral imperfection. Roger Williams would have added that although human beings in their moral incapacity must sometimes take sides against what is the greater evil, God does not act in "worldly policy" as anyone's commander in chief.

Roger Williams was indeed ahead of his time, and during the debates over the Constitution many people had not yet been persuaded to his views. On the other hand, many religious leaders had been. By 1787 they were as fully convinced as Thomas Jefferson that a firm line of division needed to be drawn between the affairs of churches and the affairs of government. We shall return to their story in a later chapter. First, we must examine the historical background of other sorts of ideas, ones not devoid of religion but more secular than the ones that inspired Williams, that led to a rejection of the model of government provided by the Christian commonwealth and the substitution for it of the godless Constitution.

CHAPTER FOUR

THE ENGLISH ROOTS
OF THE SECULAR STATE

THE MEN WHO drafted the Constitution in 1787 were not only familiar with American religious ideas and history; they were thoughtful worldly men equally well versed in the intellectual currents sweeping through the Anglo-American world. Of the fifty-five delegates in Philadelphia nearly 60 percent had attended college, a strikingly large percentage in an age when few did. Nine had gone to Princeton, four to Yale, and three to Harvard. Virtually all the delegates had family or commercial connections in England and were at home with English ideas and politics. For over two decades, in fact, from the resistance to the Stamp Act through independence and the war with Britain, American political leaders had hurled the central idea of English liberalism, the defense of individual human rights against tyrannical government, back at George III, his state ministers, and his Parliament. The source of the colonists' oppression, England, was also the source of the intellectual arsenal Americans used against her in the revolutionary era. It should be no surprise, then, that behind the godless Constitution crafted by the framers were ideas about church and state borrowed from the mother country. Nowhere is this more evident than in what the founding fathers meant by tyranny.

In the less well-known passages of his Declaration of Independence, Thomas Jefferson offered a long list of "oppressive measures" and "repeated injuries and usurpations" to prove that George III sought the "establishment of an absolute tyranny over these states." "Tyranny" is the key word here. It is a word full of emotive force in American political culture, and at our founding it is the emancipation from the tyranny of George III and his Parliaments that is enshrined in America's basic document. So pervasive is the theme that one is not surprised when visiting the beautiful Jefferson Memorial in Washington today to see emblazoned on its rotunda other memorable words of Thomas Jefferson—"I have sworn upon the altar of God eternal hostility against every form of tyranny over the mind of man."

These words of Jefferson were intended by the memorial's designers in 1943 to convey America's enduring commitment, as a religious people, to oppose vigilantly political oppression and tyranny in all its forms—be it that of George III, German kaisers, Hitler, or Japanese aggressors. But political tyranny, it turns out, was not what Jefferson intended by those words; it was religious tyranny. Neither George III nor even Louis XVI was the tyrant referred to in the original Jeffersonian passage. The line "I have sworn upon the altar of God eternal hostility against every form of tyranny over the mind of man" is from a letter written in 1800 by Jefferson to his Philadelphia friend Benjamin Rush, the distinguished physician, in the midst of Jefferson's race for president that year against the Federalist John Adams. One Federalist strategy in the campaign was, as we shall see, to smear Jefferson as an infidel because of his past connections to the French revolutionaries. A vote for Jefferson, his opponents warned, was a vote for atheism, fanatical leveling, and Jacobin frenzy. So bitter was the campaign that Jefferson sat it out in the calm of his beloved Monticello. Benjamin Rush wrote to Jefferson noting that the clergy in Philadelphia had in their sermons the preceding Sunday attacked Jefferson with claims that his election would undermine their preeminent position in American life. Jefferson's complete reply to Rush reads, "They [the clergy] believe that any portion of power confided to me, will be exerted in opposition to their schemes. And they believe rightly: for I have sworn upon the altar of God, eternal hostility against every form of tyranny over the mind of man. But this is all they have to fear from me: and enough too in their opinion."

It may shock Americans today that Jefferson in this passage, singled out for pride of place in the Jefferson Memorial, was in fact attacking the clergy of Philadelphia, the city where American freedom was born, but it would not have surprised his contemporaries. To the eighteenth-century liberal mind of a Thomas Jefferson, shaped by English ideals, there were two great sources of tyranny—kings, such as mad George III, and priests, such as the clergy of Philadelphia.

The founders of the United States like Jefferson were continuing a struggle begun in Britain in the seventeenth century to emancipate the individual from all forms of tyranny. We note in our history books, as a hallmark of this struggle, America's emancipation from the political tyranny and the economic tyranny of Britain. But we have lost sight of how important the liberal founders of America considered emancipation from what many of them saw as the equally strong menace of religious tyranny, just as we have lost sight of the English origins of this quest. That the founders of America sought economic laissez-faire, freeing the economy from state intervention, especially in the wake of a decade of oppressive taxation from London, we know well. We are less familiar with their concern for religious laissez-faire, freeing religious life from state interference, a concern that paralleled the one that drove Roger Williams but that reflected different assumptions and experiences. The Anglo-American eighteenth-century liberal championed religious freedom but joined that cause to the struggle for political and economic freedom.

We speak of liberals, by the way, in the formal sense in which historians and scholars refer to those who emphasize individual freedom in politics, in the economy, and in intellectual and religious matters as liberals. For these historical liberals, like the American founders, the state was best kept out of people's houses, out of the marketplace, and out of spiritual life. That government was best which governed least, as Jefferson put it. The word "liberal" would in the twentieth century come to be associated in post–New Deal America with non-laissez-faire advocacy of a greater state role in the economy, but the more traditional use of the word lives on in claims by a person like Milton Friedman that he is the real or true liberal, and in the labeling of opponents of governmental censorship, like the American Civil Liberties Union, as liberals.

The seedbed of this liberal world view was English political thought in the seventeenth century. The English Civil War at midcentury gave rise to a process in which political tyranny was gradually replaced by a political system emphasizing the sacredness of individual natural rights, given by God but thereafter managed by men, and the role of popular consent and popular participation in the choosing of governments. Economic constraint on individuals and the traditional restrictions on market freedom—legislative poor laws, paternalistic government, guild, and church regulation of wages and profits—gave way gradually to a free-market society where the allocation and distribution of valuable things such as power, wealth, and fame came to be seen as the result of countless individual decisions, not of some authoritative norms set by custom, God, or ruling-class decree. We have come to call this laissez-faire, which in the nineteenth and twentieth centuries would be challenged by varieties of socialism, fascism, and interventionist welfare state ideologies. But another area of individual emancipation is equally important to the emergence of liberal ideas and the liberal state—the freeing of the individual from intellectual restraint, most emphatically represented for the sixteenth, seventeenth, and eighteenth centuries as religious tyranny.

The English liberal ideal that embraced religious laissez-faire turned the Christian commonwealth ideal that had been taught by Saint Paul, Saint Augustine, Aquinas, John Calvin, and the American Puritans who banished Roger Williams into a form of tyranny. This traditional Christian view of the state, which the American founders rejected and the Christian right is dusting off today, fuses religion and politics by making the state part of God's design to redeem humanity. Its purpose is the execution of God's moral laws, the protection of God's faithful, and the furthering of God's truth. God has given His creatures a revealed law through Scripture, a set of absolute and timeless principles of right and wrong, and enjoined His creatures to live lives of virtue and morality. The state's mission is to implement this godly order in a particular time and place. Its laws are to proclaim God's truths *(e.g. creationism)* and to reward the virtuous life, while punishing sin and immorality. Those who preside in the state—traditionally monarchs, lords, and magistrates and today legislators and presidents—are God's servants, His agents in this timebound realm for the realization of the moral mission. The Christian commonwealth, be it the Catholic realm for Aquinas or the Protestant realm for an eighteenth-century Anglican bishop, or Christian America for the religious right today, sees religion and politics as forever bound to each other.

Against this traditional ideal of the Christian commonwealth there arose in seventeenth- and eighteenth-century England an alternative model of the relation of church and state, one that self-consciously separated the two realms and spoke more and more of the state as purely secular in its origins, functions, and purpose. Unlike Williams, the Englishmen who promoted this new model of government were not much concerned about the purity of true religion, which in Williams's view could prosper only if government stayed out of God's business. They too, however, contributed powerfully to the ideals that triumphed in the American Constitution. The American founders confronted and rejected a politics where the state church proclaims the moral necessity of deference and subordination to the political rulers, and where the Christian magistrate in turn ensures that proper religious observance is enforced and sinners are punished by the secular sword that assists in the achievement of a Christian society.

One of the most influential and persuasive proponents of this English liberal view of the state was John Locke. Locke was the great seventeenth-century English philosopher whose writings most shaped the intellectual and political world view of Americans in the eighteenth century. Indeed his negative attitude to the state and his preoccupation with the sanctity of private property have continued to influence the fundamental beliefs of Americans to this day. All the important figures of the founding generation, including John Otis, John and Samuel Adams, James Madison, Thomas Jefferson, Patrick Henry, and Benjamin Franklin, were disciples of Locke. His writings shaped the sermons in the revolutionary pulpits and the editorials in revolutionary newspapers. The Declaration of Independence reads like a paraphrase of Locke's influential *Second Treatise of Civil Government*. Locke's convictions form in fact the foundation of the American political creed, according to a triumvirate of distinguished twentieth-century American scholars. For Carl Becker "the lineage is direct, Jefferson copied Locke," and for Merle Curti the "Great Mr. Locke" was "America's philosopher." Louis Hartz has summarized this scholarly consensus. "Locke," he wrote in 1955, "dominates

American political thought as no thinker anywhere dominates the political thought of a nation."

For Locke, writing in the 1670s and 1680s, the state's origin was not shrouded in the impenetrable mystery of divine gift or dispensation. The source of "the powers that be," the magistrates and monarchs that governed, was the people, who voluntarily contracted to set up governments in order to protect their natural rights to life, liberty, and property. In Locke's writings we witness the birth of liberal social theory, which posits the autonomous independent individual as the center of the social universe, for whom social and political institutions are self-willed constructs whose purpose and function are to secure the rights and interests of self-seeking individuals.

In liberal Lockean social theory the function of government is purely negative. It is willed into being by individual men to serve merely as an umpire in the competitive scramble for wealth and property. Government only protects life, liberty, and property. It keeps peace and order in a voluntaristic, individualistic society. In Locke's writings government no longer seeks to promote the good or moral life. No longer does government nurture and educate its subjects in the ways of virtue, or preside over the betterment or improvement of men and society. No longer does government defend and propagate moral and religious truths. These former noble purposes of the Christian state are undermined as liberal theory assigns it the very mundane and practical role of protecting private rights, especially property rights. Two thousand years of thinking about politics in the West is overturned in Locke's writings, as the liberal state repudiates the classical and Christian vision of politics.

The state is now seen as merely the servant or agent of the propertied men who contract to set it up. Their interest in creating the state was the very worldly one of having it protect their lives, liberty, and property. The state, according to Locke, should do no more, no less. It was, as liberals would call it, a strictly limited state. If it did more, such as prescribing religious truth, or if it did less, such as failing to protect the liberty or property of its subjects, then as a mere servant it would be dismissed by those who had set it up and would be replaced by another. Such, indeed, was the political ideology of the founding fathers as captured by Jefferson in his Declaration of Independence. The language is pure Locke.

> We hold these truths to be self evident, that all men are created equal, that they are endowed by their Creator with certain unalienable rights; that among these are Life, Liberty and the pursuit of Happiness: That to secure these rights Governments are instituted among men, deriving their just powers from the consent of the governed; that whenever any form of government becomes destructive of these ends, it is the right of the people to alter or to abolish it, and to institute new Government, laying its foundation on such principles and organizing its power in such form, as to them shall seem most likely to effect their safety and happiness.

Since the liberal vision of the state assumed that it does nothing but the strictly limited chore of protecting rights, liberal theory self-consciously strips government and the state of any moral or religious function. Once again it was the Englishman John Locke who provided the principal expression of this new liberal world view for the founders, in his *Letter Concerning Toleration.* In the *Letter* Locke sought, as he put it, "to distinguish exactly the business of civil government from that of religion, and to settle the just bounds that lie between the one and the other." He does this by making clear what the state does. The state, he writes,

> seems to me to be a society of men constituted only for the procuring, preserving, and advancing their own civil interests. Civil interest I call life, liberty, health, and indolence of body; and the pos-

session of outward things, such as money, lands, houses, furniture, and the like. It is the duty of the civil magistrate, by the impartial execution of equal laws, to secure unto all the people in general, and to every one of his subjects in particular the just possession of these things belonging to this life.

In short, according to Locke, men have contracted to obey civil authority not in order for that authority to tell them what to believe or how to pray but simply for it to keep the peace. As for changing or influencing what people believe, Locke writes,

Every man has commission to admonish, exhort, convince another of error, and, by reasoning, to draw him into truth; but to give laws, receive obedience, and compel with the sword, belongs to none but the magistrate. And upon this ground, I affirm that the magistrate's power extends not to the establishing of any articles of faith, or form of worship, by the force of his laws.

This is a critical turning point in Western culture as liberal ideology, very much influenced by Protestant conviction, pushes morality and religion outside the public political realm to a private realm of individual preference. The entire definition of what is public and what is private is being changed. The public realm, which for nearly two millennia was all-inclusive, supervising in the name of the Christian commonwealth political, economic, and religious matters, has been severely curtailed as liberal theory expands the role of the private realm, giving it morality, religious belief, and soon economic activity. What a revolution the liberals achieve in insisting that matters of religious conviction are not public and political matters but private and personal ones! As Locke notes,

Any one may employ as many exhortations and arguments as he pleases, towards the promoting of another man's salvation. But all force and compulsion are to be forborne. Nothing is to be done imperiously. Nobody is obliged in that matter to yield obedience unto the admonitions or injunctions of another, further than he himself is persuaded. Every man in that has the supreme and absolute authority of judging for himself. And the reason is because nobody else is concerned in it, nor can receive any prejudice from his conduct therein.

Behind this repudiation by Locke and the founders, who were his disciples, of the assumptions of the Christian commonwealth lay pragmatic considerations as well as intellectual convictions. Millions of Europeans had died in the two centuries of religious wars between Protestants and Catholics that followed Martin Luther's break from Rome that began in Wittenberg, Germany, in 1517. The toleration of religious diversity and the rendering of religion into a matter of private conscience instead of public creed would produce domestic peace, in which no small gain would be the capacity of individuals to enjoy their rights to private property more securely. Religious strife threatened the free workings of the marketplace and the potential for self-realization through economic activity, values central to the liberalism of Locke and the founders. The rise of Protestantism ushered in forever the new reality of religious pluralism in the West, and Lockean liberalism wisely and prudently responded by dissociating religion and politics in order to keep the peace.

Behind the acceptance of toleration also lay intellectual conviction. All social institutions—the state, religion, and churches—were seen by Locke and the founding fathers as the voluntary creations of contracting individuals who set them up to serve their own interests. No longer did one receive or inherit institutions from God or the past, to which one was bound for life. So Locke could write in a magnificent rendering of Protestant dogma as liberal social theory:

Let us now consider what a church is. A church, then, I take to be a voluntary society of men, joining themselves together of their own accord in order to the public worshipping of God in such manner as they judge acceptable to Him, and effectual to the salvation of their souls. I say it is a free and voluntary society. Nobody is born a member of any church. . . . No man by nature is bound unto any particular church or sect but everyone joins himself voluntarily to that society in which he believes he has found that profession and worship which is truly acceptable to God. The hope of salvation, as it was the only cause of his entrance into that communion, so it can be the only reason of his stay there. For if afterwards he discover anything either erroneous in the doctrine or incongruous in the worship of that society to which he has joined himself, why should it not be as free for him to go out as it was to enter?

The church thus had no special or central place in the secular politics of the founders' liberalism. It was but one of many different voluntary associations in which people spent time and to which they belonged as a matter of free choice, like social clubs, Masonic lodges, and trade associations. No surprise, then, that the Protestant liberals of the seventeenth and eighteenth centuries would see marriage as a purely voluntary and contractual enterprise and would introduce marriage and especially divorce, the disavowing of contract, as civil acts.

Equally profound in this liberal revolution of the eighteenth century was the change in the understanding of what law was and what purpose it served. Pushed aside was the Christian conception of law as a worldly injunction requiring virtuous and moral living, ultimately traceable to God's own standards of right and wrong. For Locke and for the secular liberals who wrote the American Constitution, "laws provide simply that the goods and health of subjects be not injured by the fraud and the violence of others." Locke adds, "The business of law is not to provide for the truth of opinion, but for the safety and security of the commonwealth and of every particular man's goods and persons. The truth is not taught by law, nor has she any need of force to procure her entrance into the minds of men."

In this liberal revolution, this rendering private of so much that hitherto had been seen as the public role of politics, a religious establishment was the principal victim. The liberals of America's founding generation rejected the ideal of the Christian state. They saw the state a secular institution uninterested in men's souls, for, as Locke noted, the state is not concerned with matters of belief, because "no injury is thereby done to anyone, no prejudice to another man's goods." But this liberal vision of a secular state and a wall of separation between a minimal public realm, keeping the peace, and a vast private realm of moral, religious, and economic diversity and voluntarism, did not immediately and totally triumph. In the era of the American Revolution itself, a most important confrontation took place in England between the entrenched advocates of the older Christian commonwealth ideal and liberals calling for a secular state, a debate that had a profound impact in 1787 on the drafters of the godless Constitution. The fight was over the fairness of discriminatory laws that prohibited all non-Anglicans from holding public office in England. Defending these laws, conventionally referred to as the Test and Corporation Acts, against efforts in the 1770s and 1780s to repeal them were theorists of the Christian commonwealth like Edmund Burke and attacking them were liberal dissenters like Joseph Priestley and James Burgh, two men who wielded tremendous influence over America's founding fathers. So important is the story of the Test and Corporation Acts to understanding the Constitution's commitment to the separation of church and state that we must turn to it here.

The Test and Corporation Acts were passed in 1673 during the Stuart Restoration and were originally directed at Catholics. These laws required that all holders of civil or military offices under the British crown receive the sacrament according to the rites of the Anglican Church. The acts excluded nonsubscribers to the Anglican creed from any local office in an incorporated municipality, as well. In addition, the acts prohibited non-Anglicans from matriculating at Oxford or Cambridge. The Test and Corporation Acts were in effect, therefore, official governmental tests of religious correctness. The main victims of these discriminatory laws in eighteenth-century England were the Protestant dissenters—the non-Anglican Protestant sects that included Baptists, Presbyterians, Independents, Congregationalists, Unitarians, and Quakers—all with close connections to fellow churchmen in America. These dissenters made up only 7 percent of the English population but, like many marginal groups, formed an incredibly talented and successful group at the forefront of achievement. Dissenters were the leading entrepreneurs, inventors, scientists, and intellectuals during the early years of the industrial revolution. James Watt, Josiah Wedgwood, Tom Paine, and Mary Wollstonecraft, for example, were all dissenters. By the late eighteenth century these achievers lashed out at the Test and Corporation Acts, which denied them, because of their religion, access to one of the most important means a society has to reward its successful people—public office. From 1772 to 1792 the dissenters vainly sought to get through Parliament a repeal of the acts, efforts watched closely by their religious brethren in America.

The most outspoken defender of the Test and Corporation Acts and, in turn, outspoken proponent of the doomed Christian commonwealth was Edmund Burke. The great critic of the French Revolution feared that the repeal of these religious laws in England would mark the beginning of an English revolution that would make the French pale by comparison. In his speeches and writings Burke touched on all the pre- and anti-liberal themes of the Christian commonwealth ideal. He flatly rejected the liberal theory of the state. For Burke the state was much more than a Lockean voluntary artifact set up by contracting individuals bent on protecting their lives and their goods, as secular liberals argued. It had nobler and grander origins and purposes.

Religion, for Burke, was central in "the consecration of the state." The state, willed by God, is sacred because it is endowed with morality. With an established church, the state is both itself moral and the arbiter of morality. Burke insists that "in a Christian commonwealth the church and state are one and the same thing, being different integral parts of the same whole." Power and law serve God's moral design. Burke writes, "He who gave our nature to be perfected by our virtue, willed also the necessary means of its perfection—He willed therefore the state." Law severed from God and morality is, according to Burke, the "offspring of cold hearts and muddy understandings." Liberals misunderstand the nature of law. For them "laws are to be supported only by their own terrors, and by the concern, which each individual may find in them, from his own private speculations, or can spare to them from his own private interests."

Religion is a solemn responsibility of the magistrate, Burke told Parliament in 1792. It is, in words that have been echoed in American politics during the 1990s, the "great bond of society." The magistrate's role is "to protect it, promote it, and forward it." It is, he argued, the great sin of the Enlightenment, of liberals in general, and of the French Revolution in particular, that they would sever this holy connection between the church and the state. It was to prevent this from happening in England that Burke successfully led the parliamentary fight against the repeal of the Test and Corporation Acts in 1789, 1790, and 1792.

Leading the other side was the chemist Joseph Priestley, who was, according to Burke, the "patriarch" of those who "threaten the basic principles of the Christian Commonwealth wherein the church and state are one and the same." This great scientist, who discovered oxygen in 1774, was in his day much more widely known as a theologian and political radical. A founder of Unitarianism, Priestley emerged as the major spokesman for the British Protestant dissenting sects in the 1780s and 1790s and led their campaign for the repeal of the Test and Corporation Acts, as well as for the general disestablishment of the Anglican Church of England. Priestley was so popularly identified with these causes that a conservative mob burned his house and laboratory in 1791, forcing him to flee England and settle for the last ten years of his life in Northumberland, Pennsylvania, where he is buried today. Even before he emigrated to America, Priestley was a close friend and correspondent of Franklin and Jefferson. He was an important influence, along with Locke, on their secular reading of the state. Jefferson wrote to his friend Priestley in welcoming him to America, "Yours is one of the few lives precious to mankind for the continuance of which every thinking man is solicitous."

In his critique of the Test and Corporation Acts, Priestley began with the very secular liberal view of the state that Burke despised. He developed even more self-consciously than Locke the theory of the negative state, so familiar to Americans. The state no longer has any positive role to educate, nurture, or provide moral standards. It has only the specific, limited, and negative functions implicit in its contractual origins. Its sole purpose is to safeguard individuals and their rights. It is simply an agent performing the useful but limited service of keeping order and protecting individuals from harm.

The state, according to Priestley, has no authority to legislate tests of religious correctness. It deals only with "things that relate to this life," while the church deals only with "those that relate to the life to come." The state, then, is restricted to a specific purpose. It does no more or no less than provide a "secure and comfortable enjoyment of this life, by preventing one man from injuring another in his person or property." The magistrate has no concern with opinions or beliefs. His sole duty, according to Priestley, "is to preserve the peace of the society." The state punishes only "if I break the peace of society, if I injure my neighbor, in his person, property or good name," not if I believe in different creeds. "How," Priestley asks, "is any person injured by my holding religious opinions which he disapproves of?" If the answer is that such opinions endanger the salvation of others, it is still inappropriate for the state to interfere, for its "business is with the things of this life only." Priestley excludes the state from religious life, then, because it is a use of civil power beyond the limited terms of the state's contractual base. For early liberals like Locke, Priestley, and the founding fathers, the separation of church and state becomes, in fact, the crucial defining feature of liberal politics. What right does the state or anyone else have to involve itself in my religion, Priestley asks Burke in an exchange in 1791. "Does my conduct in this respect injure them? What, then, has the state, or my neighbors, to do in this business, any more than with my food or my medicine?"

An important ally of Priestley's in attacking the Test and Corporation Acts was the Scottish dissenting minister and political writer James Burgh. It is difficult to understand today how influential Burgh's books were for Americans in the age of the Revolution, but in 1790 when Jefferson advised a friend on the best writers or books on politics he listed Adam Smith, Montesquieu, "Locke's little book on government," the *Federalist,* and Burgh's *Political Disquisitions.* John Adams set himself to make Burgh's writings "more known and attended to in several parts of America" since they were "held in high estimation by all." For the modern Harvard historian Bernard Bailyn, Burgh's *Political Disquisitions* was the "key book of this [revolutionary] generation."

Burgh found the discriminatory Test and Corporation Acts a fundamental violation of Lockean secular liberal ideals. How or whether one takes communion is irrelevant in the civil sphere.

"Away with all foolish distinctions about religious opinions," he wrote; "those with different religious views are both equally fit for being employed in the service of our country." The religious legislation poses "cruel restraints on our conscience." Burgh also absorbed the Lockean voluntaristic and contractual theory of the state. What states do, Burgh contended, is merely serve the interests of those who consent to their creation. They protect well-being and property. They do not sponsor virtue and morality or further any faith.

Burgh played an important role in shaping American attitudes to the state and the place of religion in public life. He is, in fact, the original source of the metaphor, which Jefferson would use, that captures in a phrase this entire liberal secular view of the relationship between politics and religion—the wall of separation. In his book *Crito,* published in London in 1767 and widely read in America, Burgh suggested that it was essential to "build an impenetrable wall of separation between things sacred and civil." Decades before Jefferson, Burgh had offered the metaphoric alternative to the Christian commonwealth.

The Test and Corporation Acts were finally repealed in England, but not until 1829, though religious tests remained in place for admission to Oxford and Cambridge until 1871, and, of course, the Anglican Church has remained the formal established church in England to this day. In America, as we have seen, the Constitution of 1787 meant to put an end forever to religious tests in the national government, and no small credit goes to the constitutional framers' sensitivity to their dissenter brethren's exclusion from public office in England. The "no religious test" clause in the Constitution spoke with the authority of very painful recent history. America thus represented the first realization of the liberal secular vision of the separation of church and state and the first formal repudiation of the Christian commonwealth. America's founding saw the triumph, in other words, of the privatization of religion, its removal from the public realm, and its transfer to the private world of individual freedom of conscience, belief, and practice.

It is important to remember, also, that this removal of government and the state from issues of religion and morality, this victory of intellectual and religious laissez-faire, was paralleled by the victory of laissez-faire in the economy as well, the general removal of economic issues from the public realm of government and the state to a private realm of free and individual capitalist competition. It is crucial that these two developments be recognized as part of the same historical transformation—the laissez-faire liberal revolution, which has as its ideal the individual privately praying and privately acting in moral matters, free of public interference, as well as privately deciding what he should charge or what he should pay his workers, equally free from public interference. There is a logical consistency to this revolution. As matters of religion and conscience were beyond the sphere of tyrannical magistrates, so were economic matters. No surprise, then, that liberals like Priestley and Jefferson (as we shall see) were committed equally to economic and to religious laissez-faire.

Priestley's writings, for example, offer a veritable hymn to these two kinds of laissez-faire. His *Letters on History and General Policy* suggests that when a country's legislature interferes with commerce, "commerce has suffered in consequence of it." Politicians, statesmen, and even merchants themselves are ignorant of the nature of that trade. He wrote, "Most politicians have injured commerce by restricting, confining or burdening it too much." Just as he urged the end of state tests interfering with individual religious liberty, so Priestley suggested we listen to the advice of the old merchant "who being consulted . . . about what he [the magistrate] should do in favor of trade said, *Laissez nous faire* [Leave us to ourselves]." Priestley recommended Adam Smith's *Wealth of Nations* to his students and congregation and like him lashed out at mercantile restrictions on free trade. Exclusive privileges and monopolistic powers in corporations and guilds are wrong. So are tariffs and "all the laws which impede the alienation of land, or of any other commodity." Priestley was at one with Smith in arguing that "it is the highest impertinence and presumption in kings and ministers, to pretend to watch over the economy of private peoples." Individualism is as crucial in the economic as in the religious realm, Priestley insisted. Man should be "left to himself." All the restrictions on individuals should be undone so that they can "revert to that natural condition of free men from which we have departed."

So what have we seen? We have seen that the very same people, the very same English and American liberals calling for an end to the role of the church in the state with the cry of individual freedom of conscience and a limited state, were calling for an end to the role of the state in the economy, again in the name of individual freedom. Such was the nature of the victory that laissez-faire liberalism sought and achieved. In the name of individualism and freedom, all restraint, be it religious, political, or economic, was deemed tyrannical. The United States was born at a moment in Western history when emancipatory fervor sought to free individuals from the restraint of both the medieval Christian commonwealth and the medieval mercantilist economy. The religious right today wants only half of the laissez-faire ideal to which the founders of this country adhered. They accuse those we call liberals today of abandoning the founders' faith in economic laissez-faire, and there is much truth to this accusation. But they themselves have abandoned the other half of our founders' ideals, religious laissez-faire, in the name of a restored religious tyranny, the religious correctness of a revived Christian commonwealth.

In pursuing this crusade, the religious right does great disservice to the framers of the Constitution, who designed a government indifferent to guarding and promoting moral or religious truths. Politics, as they saw it, was not designed to shape virtuous character through religion. They rejected the central premise of the Christian commonwealth and in its stead created a secular state, where individuals pursued happiness as they personally conceived it, free of state tutelage and interference. Religion was a vital matter, but it was a matter of individual conscience, outside the state's concern and competence.

The framers were writing into America's fundamental law the Lockean liberal ideal. They created a demystified state, stripped of all religious ambitions. It would not serve the glory of God; it would merely preside over the commercial republic, an individualistic and competitive America preoccupied with private rights and personal autonomy. Locke had in his *Second Treatise* described the state as nothing more than "an impartial judge" or "umpire," a neutral arbiter among the competing private interests of civil society. Madison, the principal architect of the Constitution, completely shared this secular vision of the state. In his famous *Federalist* No. 10 he outlined the clashing commercial groups in America: creditors, debtors, farmers, manufacturers, merchants, and financiers. The state's purpose, he wrote, was "the regulation of these various and interfering interests," not proclaiming God's truths or rewarding a virtuous, godly life. In a 1787 letter to Washington, Madison actually described the state as being no more than a "disinterested and dispassionate umpire in disputes." Dead and buried are the lofty ambitions of the Christian state.

Among America's founders, no one better captured this moment of liberal ascendance when religious laissez-faire went hand in hand with the triumph of economic laissez-faire than Jefferson did. The basic liberal principle of the minimal state and freedom of religious expression is offered in beautiful American language by Jefferson in his *Notes on the State of Virginia,* where he explains why the state must remain unconcerned with private religious belief or even disbelief: "The legitimate powers of government extend to such acts only as are injurious to others. But it does me no injury for my neighbor to say There are twenty gods, or no God. It neither breaks my leg, nor picks my pocket." The lineage is direct. The words are strikingly similar. Locke wrote that secular laws were intended only to provide that "the goods and health of subjects be not injured." He insisted that "if a Roman Catholic believes that to be really the body of Christ, which another man calls bread, he does no injury thereby to his neighbors." Priestley asked, "How is any person injured by my holding religious opinions which he disapproves of?" The liberal laissez-faire thinkers who influenced and created America wanted religion out of politics because politics was not about salvation, or about doctrinal purity, or even about leading virtuous or moral lives. Politics was about economics and property, and the state's job was merely to be an umpire ensuring a peaceful and secure arena of economic life. It made certain that no one's leg was broken or purse stolen. For the state to do more, to involve itself in the economy or in religion, was to introduce Jefferson's dreaded tyranny— the violation of the sacred liberal maxim of "laissez nous faire." So it is to Jefferson's towering role in our story that we now turn.

CHAPTER FIVE

THE "INFIDEL"
MR. JEFFERSON

RUNNING FOR PRESIDENT in 1800, Thomas Jefferson was vilified as anti-Christian with a viciousness that rivals the attacks on President William Jefferson Clinton by the Christian right today. Bill Clinton publicly complained in a telephone call from *Air Force One* to a radio talk show. Thomas Jefferson privately wrote to a friend, "The floodgates of calumny have opened upon me." Not that the author of the Declaration of Independence had not been maligned by the clergy before. When Jefferson had become vice president in 1797, the Reverend Jedidiah Champion of Litchfield, Connecticut, closed a public prayer with "O, Lord: wilt Thou bestow upon the Vice President a double portion of Thy grace, for Thou knowest he needs it." Why he needed it was spelled out by the Reverend Timothy Dwight, president of Yale College, in a Fourth of July oration in 1798. Why, he asked, should religious people support "the philosophers, the atheists and the deists" like Jefferson? Is it so the vice president can inflict upon the nation the sins of the French Revolution, Dwight wondered, delivering a smear equivalent then to a charge today of espousing secular humanism or godless socialism.

Is it that our churches may become temples of reason, our sabbath a decade, and our Psalms of praise Marseilles hymns? Is it that we may change our holy worship into a dance of Jacobian frenzy and that we may behold such a strumpet personating a goddess on the alter of JEHOVAH? Is it that we may see the Bible cast into a bonfire? . . . Shall our sons become the disciples of Voltaire and the dragoons of Marat?

It was in the heated presidential race of 1800, between Jefferson and John Adams, that the floodgates of Christian anger opened upon Jefferson in a concerted effort to paint him as a "French infidel" and a "howling atheist." The Reverend William Linn, a Dutch Reformed minister in New York, wrote a pamphlet opposing Jefferson because of "his disbelief of the Holy Scriptures; or in other words his rejection of the Christian Religion and open profession of Deism." If this "opposer of Christianity" were elected president, Reverend Linn warned, it would have dire consequences for America. It would "destroy religion, introduce immorality and loosen all the bonds of society." Another New York clergyman, Dr. John Mason, dreaded the election of Mr. Jefferson because he believed him "to be a confirmed infidel." He works against God's word, Mason warned, and lacks "so much as a decent respect for the faith and worship of Christians." Pulpits rang with the cry that electing an infidel to the first magistracy would be "no less than rebellion against God." As an anonymous preacher put it in the *New England Palladium,*

Should the infidel Jefferson be elected to the Presidency, the seal of death is that moment set on our holy religion, our churches will be prostrated, and some infamous prostitute, under the title of Reason will preside in the sanctuaries now devoted to the worship of the Most High.

A pamphlet circulated by "A Christian Federalist" put the issues in even more dire terms:

Can serious and reflecting men look about them and doubt, that if Jefferson is elected, and the Jacobins get into authority, that those morals which protect our lives from the knife of the assassin—which guard the chastity of our wives and daughters from seduction and violence—defend our property from plunder and devastation, and shield our religion from contempt and profanation, will not be trampled upon and exploded?

One of the most damning attacks on Jefferson found in the pamphlets of both the Reverends Linn and Mason deals with Jefferson's alleged "libel" on Christ. As the story goes, Jefferson and a companion riding in the country noticed a dilapidated church. The companion reported later, according to the pamphleteers, that Jefferson said, "It is good enough for him who was born in a manger." The Reverend Linn drew the lesson. "Such a contemptuous fling at the blessed Jesus, could issue from the lips of no other than a deadly foe of his name and cause." A newspaper sympathetic to Jefferson countered this smear with what it offered as the true story. Jefferson's companion, it reported, was Italian, and seeing the church, observed that Italian priests would never enter such a run-down sanctuary. Whereupon Jefferson answered, "And yet meaner places were deemed grand enough to dispense the truth in, by HIM who was born in a manger."

In 1800, as now, a heavy dose of anti-intellectualism lurked behind the attacks on religious liberalism and freethinking. Jefferson's "atheism" was directly linked to his "too theoretical and fanciful" scientific and intellectual inclinations. His presidency of the American Philosophical Society (from 1797) condemned him to many clerical enemies. He was "impractical," too caught up in "theoretic learning" and abstract speculation. He might be qualified to be a professor "but certainly not the first magistrate of a great nation." He was "carried away by systems" and a "zeal to generalise," as opposed to "proceeding, like common men of practical sense, on the slow, but sure foundation of matter of fact." His scientific interests proved Jefferson unfit to govern, for it was noted that in his writings he doubted the biblical truth of the flood and questioned the theological consensus on the earth's age. As one clergyman put it, Jefferson's "disrespect for divine revelation" and "discrediting of sacred history" disqualified him from the presidency.

Alexander Hamilton, perhaps the least religious of all the founders but a shrewd political opportunist, joined the clergymen in the spring of 1800 in their assault on Jefferson as unchristian. Surely, he wrote, there must be some "legal and constitutional step" by which the nation could "prevent an atheist in religion . . . from getting possession of the helm of state." Article 6 of the Constitution, which Hamilton earlier had championed, specifically ruled out such a religious test, so there was only one way for the Christian crusade against Jefferson to succeed, and that was offered in banner print by the *Gazette of the United States*.

THE GRAND QUESTION STATED. At the present solemn moment the only question to be asked by every American, laying his hand on his heart, is "shall I continue in allegiance to GOD— AND A RELIGIOUS PRESIDENT; or impiously declare for JEFFERSON—AND NO GOD!!!"

Well might one wonder today how the acclaimed author of the Declaration of Independence, with its invocation of a God who made all men equal, came to be so bitterly denounced in these terms in 1800, albeit unsuccessfully, since he did, after all, defeat Adams and win the election. The Christian attack on Jefferson during the election campaign was grounded in three specific aspects of Jefferson's public life: his role in securing religious freedom in Virginia, the publication of his book *Notes on the State of Virginia,* and his seven years of government service in France.

Jefferson himself saw as the major source of the attacks on him the clergy's "resentments against the Act of Virginia for establishing religious freedom." He was right. Their pamphlets and preaching repeatedly condemned the Virginia statute of 1786 for promoting "a total disregard to public worship, and an absolute indifference to religion whatever." That statute, authorship of which Jefferson proudly asked to be put on his tombstone, was the culmination of a ten-year effort by Jefferson to write the principles of John Locke into American legislation. As early as 1776 and 1777, while a delegate to the Virginia assembly, Jefferson drafted a resolution to separate church and state in Virginia. His collected papers, first published only in the 1950s, contain a set of notes for a speech he gave making his case, and they focus on an outline he prepared of Locke's argument in his *Letter Concerning Toleration.* The magistrate's power, Jefferson wrote in his notes, extends only to the protection of civil interests, body, liberty, and property, not to care of souls and salvation, which do "no injury to thee." Laws provide only "against injury from others." In his speech Jefferson faulted Locke, however, for extending religious freedom only to Protestant dissenters and not to Catholics and nonbelievers, "but where he stopped short, we may go on."

And Virginia did go on, though not in 1776 and 1777. Over the next ten years the privileged status of Anglicanism was eroded in Virginia through steady but piecemeal efforts led by Jefferson and his younger friend James Madison. In 1785, shortly after Jefferson had gone to serve as minister to France, Madison successfully led the opposition to Patrick Henry's bill to levy a tax to provide general support of all Christian churches for what he labeled their acknowledged contribution to the diffusion of knowledge, the restraint of vice, and the preservation of social peace. Sensing the time was right, Madison reintroduced Jefferson's earlier bill for religious freedom, with its comprehensive call for a total separation of church and state.

Jefferson's famous statute opens with the sentence "Almighty God hath created the mind free." No civil laws can, therefore, burden belief or opinion. The officers of government can act only when "peace and public order" are violated. Religious tests for public office or any civic obligations are forbidden. The state cannot intrude its power in any way into areas of the mind and its principles even "on supposition of their ill tendency." In a ringing rejection of religious correctness, Jefferson's statute declares "that our civil rights have no dependence on our religious opinions, any more than our opinions in physics or geometry."

The backers of Jefferson's legislation shared his desire to "go on" from Locke, rejecting an amendment seeking to add the words "Jesus Christ" to the passage about God and the free mind. Jefferson's comment in his autobiography about this effort has telling significance in light of the debate the very next year over the Constitution's "no religious test" clause. "The insertion," he wrote, "was rejected by a great majority, in proof that they meant to comprehend within the mantle of its protection, the Jew and the Gentile, the Christian and the Mohometan, the Hindoo, and the infidel of every denomination."

Jefferson's bill became law on January 16, 1786, and news of it spread quickly. In Europe it was lauded as proof that America marked the true realization of the Enlightenment and its liberal ideals. Spiritual and intellectual laissez-faire had triumphed in Virginia, where the individual mind was left alone and free. Jefferson wrote to Madison from France that the statute had been translated into French and Italian, even inserted into the new edition of the *Encyclopédie*. In terms that could only intensify the fury of his clerical opposition in 1800, Jefferson gloried in his Statute for Religious Freedom. He wrote,

It is comfortable to see the standard of reason at length erected, after so many ages during which the human mind has been held in vassalage by kings, priests, and nobles; and it is honorable for us to have produced the first legislature who had the courage to declare that the reason of man may be trusted with the formation of his own opinions.

Equally infuriating to his clerical critics in 1800 were two passages from Jefferson's 1786 book *Notes on the State of Virginia* contained in his discussion of the state's religious history. In making his Lockean claim that religion was outside the purview of government, which is interested only in actions injurious to others, Jefferson had suggested (as we noted in the last chapter) that it was not of interest to the state whether his neighbor believed in twenty gods or no God, since "it neither breaks my leg, nor picks my pocket." According to the Reverend Mason, this was an endorsement of "the morality of devils," which would break the bonds of social order and render the world a chaotic field of competition "where fiend would prowl with fiend for plunder and blood, yet atheism neither picks my pocket nor breaks my leg." The second offensive passage appears in Jefferson's argument that only reason, persuasion, and free inquiry, not governmental coercion, find and advance truth. Arguing that only error needs the support of government, while truth stands by itself, and that it was therefore advantageous that differences of religious opinion existed, Jefferson invoked the example of what he took to be the sorry history of Christianity. His cynical sentences would be thrown back at him in an angry clerical chorus in 1800. "Millions of innocent men, women, and children, since the introduction of Christianity," Jefferson wrote, "have been burnt, tortured, fined, imprisoned." What, he asked, has been the effect of this slaughter? "To make one half the world fools, and the other half hypocrites," he answered, "to support roguery and error all over the earth."

It was this strident Enlightenment rationalism, his constant juxtaposition of reason and superstition, free inquiry and religious coercion, that made Jefferson seem so dangerous a threat to his Christian enemies. He had made his pact with the devil in his lair, the hell of enlightened revolutionary France, they argued. Had he not been closely connected with the intellectuals of Paris, the philosophes, in the years he served there? Did his radical politics not reflect the leveling democratic ideals of the Jacobin? Then as now, after all, the Christian right linked its vision of a Christian America to a conservative political agenda. Did his French friends not seek to replace Christianity with the godless "cult of reason"? Jefferson, denounced as the "Virginia Voltaire" from the pulpit and in pamphlets, was accused of helping to spread the poison produced by his friend Tom Paine, whose anti-Christian *Age of Reason,* it was noted, was written in France in the early 1790s. France had turned these two heroes of 1776 into venomous servants of Satan by 1800. As in a later age it was inconceivable for "un-American" and "un-Christian" ideals to have native roots. Diabolical intellectuals were seduced by foreign sin. A South Carolina anti-Jefferson pamphlet made this very point during the election campaign:

> It was in France, where he resided nearly seven years . . . that his disposition to theory and his skepticism in religion, morals, government, acquired full strength and vigor. . . . Mr. Jefferson is known to be a theorist on politics, as well in philosophy and morals—He is a *philosophe* in the modern French sense of the word.

Enough on Jefferson as his tormentors on the Christian right depicted him in 1800. We must turn now to a more objective exploration of his views on religion in public life, of his own religiosity, and of the impact and relevance of these on nineteenth- and twentieth-century America. Jefferson was not a godless man or intrinsically antireligious. While committed to the strictest separation of church and state, to a godless politics, and thus fiercely anticlerical, he was, as we shall see, a man of deeply felt private religious conviction.

Jefferson's views on religious practice were expressions of his radical liberal individualism. Religious belief was a purely private concern. Echoing Locke, Jefferson wrote that "the care of every man's soul belongs to himself." God, who "created the mind free," formed each individual as a self-determining moral agent freely able to forge his or her own religious principles. Jefferson wrote in 1814 that religious convictions "are a subject of accountability to our God alone. I inquire after no man's and trouble none with mine; nor is it given to us in this life to know whether yours or mine, our friend's or our foe's is exactly right." So committed was Jefferson to the sovereignty of the free individual in areas of religion that he believed it was wrong "to change another's creed." He opposed missionaries who "make converts" as well as distribute Bibles to foreigners.

Religion, a private matter, thus had no public authority or public responsibilities. As it was for Locke, religion for Jefferson was utterly independent from and free of "the right of the sword by the magistrate." Nor could religion call upon the secular state to further its spiritual ends. "Our Savior," Jefferson wrote, "chose not to propagate his religion by temporal punishments or civil incapacitations." His sense of the need to separate radically the public realm of the magistrate from the private realm of religious belief led Jefferson as president to abandon the practice of his predecessors, Washington and Adams, in proclaiming fast days and thanksgivings. This would have the secular magistrate set days of prayer and devotion, a matter beyond his limited power. Such proclamations involve issues better dealt with by religious authority, he argued, "and they can never be safer than in their own hands, where the Constitution deposited it."

It was, in fact, an explanation of his refusal to declare a national fast day that elicited from Jefferson his most detailed and famous presidential statement about keeping God out of politics. Shortly after he was elected, a group of Baptists in Danbury, Connecticut, wrote the president to acknowledge their pleasure in his victory. They had long memories, treasuring Jefferson's work in the battle for religious freedom from Anglican domination in Virginia that, as we shall see, had been their cause as well. In their letter they complained to Jefferson about their treatment under the established church of Massachusetts. Jefferson had no power under the U.S. Constitution and its First Amendment to help them. But Jefferson too had a long memory and was prepared to support their complaint in language that would powerfully affect later discussions of church and state. He called upon the metaphor he had read in the English dissenter James Burgh's book *Crito* of 1767. It was vintage English liberal theory in American constitutional dress.

> Believing with you that religion is a matter which lies solely between man and his God, that he owes account to none other for his faith or his worship, that the legislative powers of government reach actions only, and not opinions, I contemplate with solemn reverence that act of the whole American people which declared that their legislature should "make no law respecting an establishment of religion, or prohibiting the free exercise thereof," thus building a wall of separation between church and state.

After his presidency Jefferson consistently stuck to his strict separationist repudiation of a Christian state. When asked in 1817 to offer a plan for public elementary schools to the Virginia legislature, he proposed among other things to exclude clergymen as school trustees and to bar religious instruction that violated the beliefs of any sect or denomination. The plan was rejected. He was more successful in his next effort to realize his vision of a godless public sphere, the creation of the University of Virginia in the 1820s. Mr. Jefferson's state university would preserve the wall of separation intact. It would be America's first truly secular university, having no religious instruction, other than as a branch of ethics, and no professor of divinity.

If English liberalism informed Jefferson's secular vision of American politics, it and the French Enlightenment lay behind the fierce anticlericalism of the "Virginia Voltaire." How shocking Jefferson's vitriolic attacks on ministers of God, especially those who meddled in politics, seem to late-twentieth-century sensibility. Christ saw no need for priests, Jefferson wrote. They were not necessary "for the salvation of souls." He suggested to John Adams, his friend after they had left politics, that "we should all, then, like the Quakers, live without an order of priests," and "moralise for ourselves, following the oracle of conscience." The *"genus irritabile vatum"* (the irritable tribe of priests) had subverted the pure morality of primitive Christianity to serve their own selfish interests, according to Jefferson. They "perverted" Christianity "into an engine for enslaving mankind, a mere contrivance to filch wealth and power to themselves." On another occasion he labeled this as the priestly quest for "pence and power," which "revolts those who think for themselves." The clergy stood condemned, along with monarchy and the nobility, as the people's enemies. Like kings and aristocrats "in every country and in every age," Jefferson wrote, "the priest has been hostile to liberty. He is always in alliance with the despot, abetting his abuses in return for protection to his own."

Priests were the subverters of reason and enlightenment, for centuries duping decent Christians into "burning and torturing one another for abstractions which no one of them understand." They weave "spells" for their flocks, "moulding their minds as wax in the hollows of their hands." All priests, Jefferson claimed, "dread the advance of science as witches do the approach of daylight." They preach "bigotry and fanaticism" at the expense of human reason. "The mountebanks calling themselves the priests of Jesus" spread "impenetrable darkness . . . and there they will skulk." A "band of dupes and impostors," they sponsor "ignorance, absurdity, untruth, charlatanism and falsifications."

His historical reading of clerics was only reinforced by their attacks on him in 1800. Writing to a friend, Jefferson confided that he was not afraid of priestly attacks. They had tried "all their various batteries of pious whining, hypocritical canting, lying and slandering, without being able to give me one moment of pain." American clergymen were no different from the "mystery mongers" of Europe. Writing of Congregational ministers in New England, Jefferson complained that "no mind beyond mediocrity dares to develop itself there" where they have gotten "a smell of union between church and state." He was thrilled in 1818 when the Presbyterian Church was removed as Connecticut's established church, writing to John Adams about "the resurrection of Connecticut to light and liberty." He applauded Adams and all New England now "that this den of priesthood is at length broken up, and that a protestant popedom is no longer to disgrace American history and character." Nor was Jefferson any less harsh on the Presbyterian clergy of Virginia who condemned his godless university. They were, he wrote, "the most tyrannical and ambitious, ready at the word of the lawgiver to put the truth to the pile. . . . They pant to re-establish by law, that holy inquisition, which they can now only infuse into public opinion."

Outspokenly anticlerical and vigilant to exclude religion from public life as he may have been, Jefferson was, it must be emphasized, not himself a godless man. He was in fact living proof of his own argument that religion as private conviction could flourish without public endorsement. He attended church services in Washington and Charlottesville and contributed money frequently to Episcopal, Presbyterian, and Baptist churches. He talked and wrote in private about his own personal religious beliefs and was far from being the impious atheist and infidel depicted by his detractors. He believed fervently in the one God who had created all men equal. While never formally abandoning the Episcopalianism of his Virginia youth, he usually identified himself as a Unitarian. In this respect he was deeply influenced by the writings of his scientific friend the Reverend Joseph Priestley. They both rejected the Trinity as a "metaphysical insanity" and shared the general deistic rejection of the miracles of the Bible, the divinity of Christ, and the doctrines of original sin and blood atonement. Jefferson, in fact, predicted that one day in a rational America everyone would be a Unitarian. But Jefferson differed dramatically from the coldly rational deism and Unitarianism of Priestley in his passionate preoccupation with Jesus as the focus of a truly moral Christianity.

Far from being one of "the bitterest enemies of Christ," as the Reverend Mason claimed in 1800, Jefferson embraced a personal religion shaped by the life and teachings of Jesus. He called his own creed "the philosophy of Jesus" and referred often to "the purity and sublimity of his moral precepts." Christ was, according to Jefferson, "the greatest teacher of moral truths that ever lived." In Jesus' life and teachings, Jefferson wrote to Adams, could be found "the most sublime and benevolent code of morals which has ever been offered to man." He emphasized the Sermon on the Mount and Jesus' call to men to love all mankind. In Christ's teaching "that to love God with all thy heart and thy neighbor as thy self, is the sum of religion," Jefferson wrote.

To offer witness that he was, as he put it, "a real Christian, that is to say a disciple of the doctrine of Jesus," Jefferson assembled late in his career what he called his bible. He pasted together in one red morocco leather volume Greek, Latin, French, and English translations of the teachings of Jesus, adding his own commentaries and interpretations. In his handwriting he inscribed on the title page, "The Life and morals of Jesus of Nazareth." Jefferson kept his Jesus bible to himself, never publicizing his beliefs. Several close friends who knew of its existence urged him to have it published. Jefferson sympathized with their pleas that to do so would answer those clergy who called him "infidel, atheist, deist or devil." He declined, however, writing to one confidant, "I have ever thought religion a concern purely between our God and our consciences, for which we were accountable to Him, and not the priests."

It is worthwhile to note that Jefferson's views were by no means fundamental departures from those of his fellow founding fathers. He evoked much more criticism for his religious liberalism than they did because it was linked by his critics to his more radical politics and his French connections. While George Washington, for example, was, unlike Jefferson, perfectly willing to proclaim fast days and thanksgivings, he also was, as Edwin Gaustad, one of America's most distinguished historians of religion, labels him, "a cool deist." He characteristically referred to God as the "Grand Architect of the Universe" or in other terms favored by Enlightenment rationalists, including "Higher Cause," "Great Ruler of Events," "Superintending Power," "Supreme Dispenser of all Good," and "Governor of the Universe." Washington wrote proudly of his opposition to "the horrors of spiritual tyranny, and every species of religious persecution." He rejoiced in 1793 that in America "the light of truth and reason had triumphed over the power of bigotry and superstition" and that every American could worship God "according to the dictates of his own heart." Earlier, in the midst of a military expedition in Canada, General Washington had alerted Colonel Benedict Arnold to respect the free exercise of religion among the Catholic French Canadians, and not to violate "the right of conscience in others, ever considering that God alone is the judge of the hearts of men."

Washington supported Jefferson's legislative efforts to achieve religious freedom in Virginia, calling public support of Christianity "impolitic." Even more significant was his support of the Constitution as godless. In 1789 a group of Presbyterian ministers and elders from Massachusetts and New Hampshire wrote to Washington, who had presided over the Constitutional Convention, complaining that the Constitution lacked any reference to "the only true God and Jesus Christ, who he hath sent." In his reply, Washington wrote that he believed "the path of true piety is so plain as to require but little political direction." Not the state and its institutions, he went on, but ministers of the gospel were to further the "advancement of true religion." That is why, he respectfully submitted, there was "the absence of any regulation respecting religion from the Magna Carta of our country."

John Adams, like Washington, had no difficulty as president with governmentally sponsored days of fasting and thanksgiving, but in other respects he, too, stood close to Jefferson in his religious views. He shared the Enlightenment's commitment to an unfettered individual reason. "Let the human mind loose," he wrote. "It must be loose. It will be loose. Superstition and dogmatism cannot confine it." Like other Enlightenment deists, he saw a rational universe "governed by intelligence and wisdom." The state was a godless institution. Americans, Adams wrote, possessed "an utter contempt of all that dark ribaldry of . . . the divine, miraculous original of government with which priesthood had enveloped the feudal monarch in clouds and mysteries." He was, though less outspoken, as anticlerical as Jefferson, and he shared the rejection of the Trinity, considering himself a Unitarian for most of his life. Interestingly enough, given his general conviction that politics and constitutions were wholly secular matters, Adams in his old age seems to have had second thoughts about having proclaimed fast days while president. "Nothing is more dreaded," he wrote in 1812, "than the national government meddling with religion."

And then there is James Madison, America's fourth president. His views on religion and politics are hard to distinguish from Jefferson's, since they were allies in the struggle for religious liberty in the early Republic. He, too, worried about that "religious bondage" which "shackles and debilitates the mind," and he, too, condemned the "infernal infamy" of the clergy with their "diabolical Hell conceived principle of persecution." He, like Jefferson, envisioned an America that "extinguished forever the ambitious hope of making laws for the human mind."

The conviction that religion lay outside the provenance of government rested for Madison, as for Jefferson, on Lockean liberalism. The purpose of the civil state, Madison wrote, was "to protect the property of every sort," which included "the rights of persons to their external goods" and to the "enjoyment and communication of their opinions." Opinions and conscience were also sacred forms of individual property, as crucial to one's sense of self as material possessions were. Government, then, according to Madison, had no more right to invade or regulate "a man's conscience" than "his castle," both of which were his "natural and unalienable rights." From these Lockean assumptions Madison forged a career as champion of strict separation between church and state, first as legislator in Virginia, then as "father of the Constitution" and the Bill of Rights, and finally as president.

Decisive in the passage of Jefferson's Statute for Religious Freedom in Virginia had been the document *Memorial and Remonstrance* that Madison had drafted and circulated to the Virginia assembly in 1785. In it he argued that religious opinions and beliefs were "not the object of civil government, nor under its jurisdiction." Reason and private conscience dictate religious conviction and "judge of religious truth"—not the public authority of politicians. If government legislated Christianity in Virginia and in America, Madison warned, the evils from which Americans fled Europe would return: "pride and indolence in the clergy, ignorance and servility in the laity; in both, superstition, bigotry and persecution." Better to leave legislating religion to "the Supreme Lawgiver of the universe," not to magistrates in the assembly. This, of course, was the very same conviction he impressed upon the delegates in Philadelphia during the summer of 1787, when as "floor manager" he helped craft the godless Constitution.

It was this set of convictions that also informed Madison's intention in drafting the religious clauses of the First Amendment. Madison had been brought around to the need for a bill of rights by his friend and mentor Jefferson, who had written from Paris endorsing the Constitution, suggesting, however, that it sorely lacked a bill of rights, one "providing clearly for freedom of religion." Madison promised Anti-Federalist opponents of the Constitution that the first Congress would amend the Constitution to include guarantees of such rights and as a member of the House of Representatives he, in fact, steered the Bill of Rights through Congress. Much controversy rages today over what Congress in 1791 intended by the two religious clauses in the First Amendment: "Congress shall make no law respecting an establishment of religion, or prohibiting the free exercise thereof." The Christian right offers a narrow reading in which the first clause refers only to the prohibition of a national church, while strict separationists read that clause more broadly, as Jefferson did in his 1802 letter to the Danbury Baptists. What is perfectly clear, despite today's debate, is that Madison, the father of the Bill of Rights, shared Jefferson's broader reading.

President Madison vetoed a bill in 1811 passed by Congress that simply gave a charter to an Episcopal church within the District of Columbia. The bill referred to the functions of this particular church in dispensing charity and education to the neighboring poor. Madison's veto claimed that the legislation violated the First Amendment and "would be a precedent for giving to religious societies as such a legal agency in carrying into effect a public and civic duty." The bill, he added, would blur, and indeed erase, "the essential distinction between civil and religious function." That same year Madison vetoed legislation that would have given federal land to a Baptist church in the Mississippi Territory. Clearly the establishment of a national church was not at issue, but Madison claimed the bill violated the First Amendment, comprising "a precedent for the appropriation of funds of the United States for the use and support of religious societies."

Madison was consistent in his broader reading of the restraints on government involvement in religion. He opposed, for example, including clergymen in the census count of trades and professions. They could not be counted, he wrote, because "the general government is proscribed from interfering, in any manner whatever, in matters respecting religion." He also opposed, unsuccessfully, the appointing of chaplains to Congress. Their payment from the national treasury, he argued, violated the First Amendment, as did the affront "to members whose creeds and consciences forbid a participation in the majority."

Madison once dramatically abandoned this strict separationism, however. When the war with Britain was declared in 1812, Congress requested a national fast day "with religious solemnity as a day of public humiliation and prayer" in support of the war. With the new nation caught in a war widely regarded as his war, Madison was under intense political pressure, as critics of the godless constitution renewed their old charges. The still powerful Timothy Dwight provided a gloomy assessment of the nation's chances in the war for students assembled in the Yale College chapel: "The nation has offended Providence. We formed our Constitution without any acknowledgement of God; without any recognition of His mercies to us, as a people, of His government, or even of His existence. The [Constitutional] Convention, by which it was formed, never asked even once, His direction, or His blessings, upon their labours. Thus we commenced our national existence under the present system, without God." In this case, Madison set aside his long-held view that it was no part of government's function to proclaim religious days and issued as nonsectarian and voluntary a proclamation as he could draft. He recommended, rather than decreed, that religious denominations and societies "so disposed" appeal to God for assistance in the war. There was no suggestion that failure to comply involved any public penalty.

In his retirement Madison came to regret his tortured distinction that governmental encouragement of prayers was somehow less unconstitutional if it was only a recommendation. By 1819 he was insisting that people had been wrong to fear "that civil governments could not stand without the prop of a religious establishment," in the debates over religious freedom in Virginia and over the ratification of the Constitution. The American experience had proved that rejecting the Christian commonwealth and effecting "a perfect separation between ecclesiastical and civil matters" could work. In 1832, at the age of eighty-one, Madison conceded that it might not be easy to keep clear the line between religious and civil authority; he had himself had problems with his war proclamation, he noted. All the more reason, then, he advised future generations, to take the strictest reading of the separation of church and state, "an entire abstinence of the government from interference in any way whatever." It was thus a clear affront to history for Chief Justice Rehnquist, in 1985 when urging that the metaphor of the wall be "frankly and explicitly abandoned," to suggest that even Madison was "obviously not a zealous believer" in the "wall of separation between church and state idea which latter-day commentators have ascribed to him."

America's historical memory of Madison's chief mentor, Jefferson, has been rooted in distinct features of his protean career. For many observers in the nineteenth and twentieth centuries, Jefferson has been the symbol of states' rights and the opposition to centralized government. To others he remains the spokesman of a radical and popular democracy never achieved in America. He is for some the tortured sensitive antebellum southerner, intellectually committed to the end of slavery, but never quite able to free his own slaves. For many he is also the quintessential American spokesman of Lockean liberalism, with its laissez-faire assumptions about individual economic freedom from government. He wrote, after all, that "agriculture, manufacture, commerce, and navigation, the four pillars of our prosperity, are the most thriving when left free to individual enterprise." In his first inaugural address he had also promised, as have so many presidents since, "a wise and frugal government which shall restrain men from injuring one another, which shall leave them otherwise free to regulate their own pursuits of industry and improvement." Not unrelated to this, of course, is Jefferson's spiritual laissez-faire, and it is also for this commitment to the individual's religious freedom from government that he is remembered, for better or for worse.

Jefferson's "irreligion" lay behind the Philadelphia public library's refusal well into the late 1830s to place any book about him on its shelves. On the other hand, the man who saved Monticello from shameful neglect after Jefferson's death, the naval hero Uriah Phillips Levy, was a Jew who acted, he said, because Jefferson had done so much "to mold our Republic in a form in which a man's religion does not make him ineligible for political or governmental life." In North Carolina, William Gaston, the Catholic who in 1836 sought to end all religious tests for public office and had to settle for substituting "Christians" for "Protestants" in the state constitution, invoked Jefferson's "imperishable manifesto of the religious rights of man."

Andrew Jackson kept high the Jeffersonian wall of separation. During a cholera epidemic in 1832, Congress was petitioned by numerous churches to proclaim a fast day and, led by Henry

Clay, it passed such a resolution. President Jackson refused to issue the proclamation, citing Jeffersonian principles. His critics attacked him for accepting the infidel Jefferson's belief "that Christianity has no connection with the law of the land." These views, foreign to the American heritage, were merely "the flippant and superficial judgement of the Virginia Voltaire," wrote Samuel D. Parker, attorney for the Commonwealth of Massachusetts in 1834. Thirty years later, during the Civil War, Horace Bushnell, the famous Connecticut preacher, saw the bloody conflict as divine retribution for America's acceptance of "the speculative and infidel" ideas that government was not sanctified by God and divinely ordained, ideas "represented in the life and immense public influence of Mr. Jefferson." Bushnell took solace, however, in Secretary of the Treasury Chase's wartime decision to put the motto "In God we trust" on the nation's money.

By the end of the century Jefferson's influence on religious issues worked in unpredictable ways. The U.S. Supreme Court, for example, quoted him to uphold Utah's prohibition of Mormon polygamy. This kind of governmental interference with religion, the Court held, was justified because, in the Lockean words of Jefferson's Virginia statute, these religious principles involved acts that injured people and disturbed "peace and public order." On the other hand, Jefferson's secular university was attacked by opponents of public higher education in the South, most notoriously in 1900 by Dr. John C. Kilgo, president of Trinity College, which was then a Methodist institution in Durham, North Carolina, patronized by the Duke tobacco family, after whom it is now named. Jefferson's university, a marriage of "civil authority and infidelity," should be a warning to southerners, Kilgo urged, that they patronize church schools. He warned the Methodist faithful not to go to the state University of North Carolina, which, he suggested, followed Jefferson's principles. Jefferson was "an infidel, agnostic, and a materialist," and his university was "a deistic daring of enormous proportions" intended to subvert Christianity. Only if churches sponsored their own universities could America be saved.

Kilgo's crusade against Jeffersonian secular education coincided ironically with the discovery of Jefferson's bible, lost since his death. Urged by an Iowa congressman, a delighted U.S. Congress voted in 1902 to publish at public expense Jefferson's life and teachings of Jesus. Despite claims that to do so would constitute "a direct, public and powerful attack upon the religion of Christians everywhere," not to mention Jefferson's wish to keep his religious views a private matter beyond government scrutiny, Congress was undeterred. The "Virginia Voltaire" was officially rehabilitated as the "real Christian" Mr. Jefferson.

Jefferson's return to public favor reached its climax during the New Deal. He was put first on a stamp and then on the nickel, and was finally given a magnificent memorial in Washington, dedicated on the bicentennial of his birth in 1943. America was then at war around the globe with the tyrannical enemies of freedom and reason. The three-member federal commission appointed in 1939 by President Roosevelt chose appropriately to grace Jefferson's memorial with his words from the Virginia statute and the Declaration of Independence. The chairman, Senator Elbert Thomas of Utah, who later wrote a book about Jefferson, chose the passage destined for the place of honor, the base of the rotunda. It was a line he thought would inspire an America locked in a worldwide combat with the forces of tyranny. Jefferson's comment from his letter to Rush—"I have sworn upon the altar of God eternal hostility against every form of tyranny over the mind of man"—was his choice, which brings us full circle back to the presidential campaign of 1800. Jefferson had the last word in his war with the clergy, and it is engraved in stone.

CHAPTER SIX

AMERICAN BAPTISTS
AND THE JEFFERSONIAN
TRADITION

THE FIERCE OPPOSITION of many churchmen that Jefferson encountered in 1800 was especially sharp in New England, where a defense of church establishment persisted the longest. Indeed, in winning the election of 1800, Jefferson carried none of the New England states. Yet, despite the attacks of the clergy, Jefferson and his fellow Republicans did very well among churchgoing Americans. He carried many of the votes of the growing number of Protestant evangelicals who had suffered discrimination and enormous condescension under the colonial church establishments. In the early nineteenth century they seized upon revivalism as the great engine of democratic church making and, in so doing, participated in a populist revolt that soon turned the Methodist and Baptist denominations into the largest by far of American Protestant church organizations. Many of the early itinerant Methodist ministers in the young American Republic proudly called themselves radical Jeffersonians. John Leland, a Baptist minister, demonstrated his appreciation of the new president by presenting Jefferson, at the White House on New Year's Day 1802, with a 1,235-pound "Mammoth Cheese." On it was written "Rebellion to tyrants is obedience to God."

These evangelicals knew, of course, that Jefferson did not share their religious convictions, but that did not matter. This chapter explores the reasons why American Baptists in 1800 were unimpressed by the Federalist criticisms of Jefferson's religious views and why they voted for him. It also compares the original Baptist stance on the matter of church-state relations with more recent pronouncements made by leaders of the Southern Baptist Convention, now the largest group of American Baptists, in fact the largest group of American Protestants. The argument will be that insofar as Southern Baptists have recently been urged by their pastors and their convention leaders to enter the world of partisan politics with the goal of using government to enforce a sectarian view of what counts as moral behavior, they stand in flagrant contrast to their forebears who risked life and reputation to "come out of the world" and create a religious society that expected nothing in religious terms from the state and dictated nothing in religious terms back to the state. The earlier Baptists got to this point without reading John Locke and without thinking about religious toleration in the same way that Thomas Jefferson did. Their story is therefore extremely important in refuting the notion that the idea of the godless Constitution is the invention of militant secularists.

Who are Baptists anyway? To ask that question is to invite a quarrel about the continuity of the primitive Christian church that need not detain us in these pages. For our purposes, Baptists first appeared in the sixteenth century as part of the Reformation ferment. In German-speaking areas their distinctive tradition of rejecting the practice of infant baptism split them apart from the forces linked to Martin Luther very early in the Reformation period. The English manifestation came later, early in the seventeenth century, when Anabaptists organized a small but vocal religious community during the reign of James I. In the American colonies, the first important chapter in the history of Baptists started in New England. Roger Williams was briefly a Baptist and organized the First Baptist Church in Providence in 1639. But Williams went on to pursue a religious quest that was more personal and anti-institutional than that advocated by most Baptists. The latter were finally able to organize a church in Boston in 1665, some ten years after Henry Dunster had been forced to step down from the presidency of Harvard College because he refused to present his child for baptism. The main growth spurt of Baptists in colonial America came in the 1740s and 1750s, during the period of the First Great Awakening. Anabaptism was not a united movement, but in all of its incarnations it formed part of the Reformation's "left wing." The label refers not only to the uncompromising religious stance of Anabaptist leaders but also to their social militancy, which sought to erase the class distinctions of the European social order. On the continent, Thomas Münzer, who was blamed for the peasants' revolt of 1525, which Luther brutally condemned, was an Anabaptist. So was Menno Simons, who founded the Mennonites, one of the many small sects of German Pietism that were to become part of the American landscape of religious pluralism. Although English Anabaptists had only vague connections to the German movement, they gained the same reputation for being social troublemakers. Partly for that reason English and American Puritans, who had their own reputation for social divisiveness to worry about, wanted nothing to do with them. American Puritans linked Baptists to Seekers, Ranters, Quakers, and Shakers. These fanatical people, it was charged, pushed the concept of religious purity so far that all constituted authority, whether religious or secular, was placed in question.

Their critics had a point, for Baptist identity crystallized around repeated challenges to the authority of governments to define and enforce proper religious belief. The Baptist challenge to the colonial authorities in New England arose because Baptist theology pointed to an embarrassing weakness in the logic of New England Puritan thought. If you believed, as did the leaders of the Massachusetts Bay Colony, that church membership ought to be restricted to people who could give evidence of being among God's chosen saints, then how could you justify the practice of allowing church members to present their newborn children for baptism? Baptists correctly pointed out that nothing in the Bible suggested the common Christian practice of infant baptism. The biblical prototype for the Catholic sacrament, Christ's baptism by John the Baptist in the river Jordan, was clearly a story about the ritual behavior of adults who were not afraid to immerse themselves in water. In fact, if people also believed, as did the New England Puritans, that God had preselected His saints (the doctrine of predestination) and that only adult behavior could give evidence that one was among the elect, then the baptism of children was perhaps a sinful act because it violated a biblical injunction. The fact that a child's parents were church members who had established a presumptive case for their election signified nothing about an infant's predestined status. Presumptive election does not run in bloodlines. In strict Calvinist theology an infant born into the world was presumed damned until proved otherwise. Infant baptism was therefore an affront to God's omnipotence and to His design for earthly churches.

By pointing to this lapse in the otherwise strict Calvinism in Puritan thinking, Baptists made themselves unwelcome in Boston. By the rules of the religious and social order established in New England, Baptists were dissenters who were at first tolerated not at all and then only in the most grudging and minimal ways. Not surprisingly, the harsh treatment American Baptists received reinforced their tendency to vent hostility toward worldly governments, and the false distinctions that governments created among human beings. Taking a view of church-state relations very different from the one fashionable in colonial America, they rejected not only the idea of one established church but even the very notion of state tax levies to support churches.

Baptists had to petition England to find any support for their grievances. From the standpoint of the English crown, the whole religious situation in New England during the seventeenth century looked very odd. The established Puritan church there, the church that all colonists had to support through a tax assessment, was not the Church of England. The American Puritans were dissenters, despite the claim of most of them that they were not separatists, and it made no sense that these dissenters, who did not yet have clear rights to free religious practice in England, presumed under English law to cut off the rights of other Protestant dissenters. After 1682 crown policy made it impossible for American Puritans in Massachusetts and Connecticut to forbid Baptists to build churches. The Puritan colonial magistrates also could no longer hang Quakers. This limited sort of tolerance, which gave no succor to Catholics or to Jews, became indelibly part of the law of the realm when England passed its Act of Toleration in 1689, following the "Glorious Revolution" and the succession of William and Mary to the throne.

Yet for the next several decades Baptists still had to pay taxes to support Congregational and Presbyterian churches. Only after 1728 did Massachusetts begin to pass laws that granted the right of Anglicans, Baptists, and Quakers to exemption from the burden of paying the bills for New England's official church. Again the pressure came from the crown and for the same reasons that had been used in 1682 to force a right to free worship for these groups. Although it made perfect sense (to the crown) that English Baptists living in England had to pay taxes to support the Church of England, no group of religious dissenters (that is, Puritan Congregationalists who rejected the authority of the English church hierarchy) had the right to tax other dissenters (Baptists) to pay for their wayward practices.

Matters were far from settled. Baptists had won an important point but within a limited context. They had successfully defended their belief that the state had no right to tax them to maintain their churches. Baptist churches were voluntary organizations that existed beyond the corrupting power of the state. Yet this principle had no force outside of New England. It did not serve as precedent for the Baptists who struggled for a foothold in the southern colonies, where the Church of England remained established. A general principle of church voluntarism had not carried the day, nor did New England's Baptists at this point seem to care. What difference did it make to them if the vast majority of the churches of New England continued to receive tax money from the state? What difference, in fact, did it make if Jews, Turks, and papists had no religious rights at all in New England? In seeking exemption for themselves, Baptists were not thinking, like Roger Williams, about the need of the state to get out of the business of religion absolutely. They had more to learn.

Always to their credit, New England Baptists profited from experience. It soon enough was clear to them that the particular tax exemption granted to them did not provide a degree of church-state separation sufficient to protect their wish to be left in peace. For one thing, their ability to gain tax exemption if they could prove that they worshiped at a Baptist church did not exempt them from social prejudice and ill treatment by their neighbors. If anything, informal abuse increased because Baptist actions appeared to be merely self-serving and therefore contemptuous of the general community. Their refusal to share a tax burden only raised the rates and the resentment of everybody else.

Moreover, Baptists had not yet cleared themselves from the interfering power of the state. To gain their tax exemption, they had to seek a formal certificate from local town officials stating that they were in fact Baptists and regularly attended a Baptist church. These certificates were not always easy to get, and disputes between Baptists and tax officials took people to court with depressing regularity. As long as the state issued the certificates, it also controlled the definition of what was or was not acceptable Baptist religious practice.

With the Great Awakening of the 1740s and 1750s the problem worsened. For the first time in New England's history, Baptists threatened to become numerous. Many Congregational Puritans who to this point had been members of the standing order were convinced by the revival fever that New England's churches had grown slack. A demand for stricter standards of membership split churches. A number of new "separate" churches formally became Baptist churches. These were not the "old" Baptists but the "separate" Baptists. New England's local tax collectors were not prepared to accept this sort of recantation without a fight, and they regularly refused to issue certificates of exemption to members of these new churches. The repercussions for people of conscience were severe. One woman who lived in Raynham, Massachusetts, refused to pay a tax of eight pence and was placed in prison for thirteen months. In 1769, Baptists in the town of Ashfield who refused to pay taxes had their land seized and sold at auction. Property whose real market value was close to four hundred pounds was grabbed up by non-Baptists for bids that in sum did not reach twenty pounds.

Isaac Backus, who separated from the Congregational Church in 1746, and John Leland, whose gift of cheese to Jefferson has been noted, emerged as the leaders of the next phase of Baptist complaints against the state. Such victories as they won did not come easily, a reality that only increased their resistance and prompted them to move their protest beyond the issue of tax exemption. They now targeted the whole system of certification.

When the events that led to the American Revolution started heating up after the passage of the Stamp Act in 1763, New England's Baptists were in something of a quandary. The victories they had won against the New England establishment had been won by appeal to the English crown. Yet their successful appeals to the mother country had never meant that English policy was especially friendly to Baptists. Baptists in Massachusetts and Connecticut knew that if they had lived in England, or for that matter in Virginia, their situation would have been worse than it was in New England. Therefore, Isaac Backus decided to throw his weight behind the patriot protesters and see what he could get by using the revolutionary rhetoric of "no taxation without representation." In 1773, the year of the Boston Tea Party, Backus sought to mobilize Baptists in direct action to protest the certificate law. He urged them to refuse as a group to turn in the certificates that gave them tax exemption and at the same time refuse to pay taxes. He meant to invite reprisals, for violation of the certificate law was punishable, as we have seen, by jail terms, public whipping, and the confiscation of property. It was time, Backus in effect said, for Baptists to burn their draft cards.

Backus's attempt to get Baptists involved in a collective protest in behalf of their rights ran smack into another strong Baptist tradition, a fierce individualism. Whatever Baptists felt about certificates, many of them were reluctant to let a vote determine, or seem to determine, their conscience. In this sense a Baptist assembly that tried to set policy for individual Baptist churches was just as potentially threatening as any state action. Backus in fact was not able to fill the jails of New England with protesting Baptists as he had hoped. He did, however, dramatically make the point that Baptists, in joining the revolutionary cause, intended to fight for religious freedom, not for some patriot's idea of a Christian commonwealth. In *An Appeal to the Public for Religious Liberty,* a tract that appeared in 1774, a Baptist author attacked the certificate law because "the very nature of such a practice implies an acknowledgment that the civil power has a right to set one religious sect against another . . . and emboldens people to judge the liberty of other men's consciences."

As it happened, the Revolution did not resolve New England Baptist grievances. True, the Massachusetts constitution that was adopted in 1780 stated that "no subordination of any one sect or denomination to another shall ever be considered by law." That phrase ended the certificate system as it had existed. However, the constitution also required that all citizens pay taxes to support the religion of their choice. That proviso meant that Baptists, who before had been allowed to support their churches voluntarily, now had to pay taxes and then negotiate with the state government about how and to whom the money was to be returned. Arguably the coercion of conscience was worse than what had existed before. Government had successfully reasserted its right to act as the guardian of religion.

Baptists argued in the *Balkcom* case, decided in 1782, that forced tax support in effect meant that the government was dictating to a religious minority a religious practice approved by a majority. Such dictation clearly subordinated one sect to another. However, this good argument, which laid down the general principle that would lead most Baptists to oppose prayer in public schools many years later, failed to convince the court. With respect to taxation, it was left to persistence to accomplish what logic could not. For all practical purposes the state of Massachusetts stopped bothering Baptists. It wasn't worth the trouble to collect religious taxes from such quarrelsome folk when the money went back to them anyway.

That was not quite the end of church establishments in the United States. The religious clauses of the First Amendment to the Constitution placed no constraints on individual states. Massachusetts stubbornly maintained the form of its religious establishment longer than any other New England state. Vermont gave it up in 1807. Connecticut followed suit in 1818 and New Hampshire in 1819. Massachusetts' tax-supported church did not disappear until 1833, and then only because the conservative Congregationalists believed that Unitarians were getting most of the benefit. Finally everyone realized that tax support unfairly subsidized those churches that showed the least potential for popular expansion.

With their colonial experience in mind, Baptists of course believed that they owed Jefferson political support in 1800. Beginning with their eager backing of Jefferson's Statute for Religious Freedom in Virginia, American Baptists gave qualified support to Jefferson's wall of separation between church and state, the phrase that Jefferson had first used in 1802 in his letter to a committee of the Danbury, Connecticut, Baptist Association. To Baptists it seemed that Jefferson had learned from his reading of English political thinkers what they had learned over many years in the efforts to promote the proper form of Christian worship: the function of government, whether democratic or undemocratic, was not to sustain or sponsor religion. Baptists agreed with Jefferson that America had not been founded as a Christian nation. Baptists in fact regarded the great majority of Americans as non-Christian. They belonged to no church. And they had never had a saving experience of God's grace.

Not everything was settled however, and in these early days of the American Republic, Baptists, like many other Americans, began to disagree about the meaning and implementation of church-state separation. That letter by Jefferson to the Danbury Baptist Association urged an end to tax-supported churches, to religious tests and to any other religious legislation. Isaac Backus deviated from Jefferson on many points. He did not seem to mind the common assertion made by people in high places, indeed by judges, that the United States was a Christian nation. At least he said nothing about a clause in the Massachusetts constitution that required officeholders to swear, "I believe the Christian religion and have a firm persuasion of its truth." He supported a further religious test clause in the Massachusetts constitution that discriminated against Roman Catholics, and he did not take up arms against unenforced New England laws that required Sunday church attendance. The intrusion of the Westminster catechism in the public schools did not bother him. Nor did state and local laws against theater going, gambling, blasphemy, and disturbing the Sabbath. Backus apparently regarded all of these things not as instances of coerced religious conscience—which they were—but as measures pertinent to decent public order that served Christians and non-Christians alike. Jefferson had said that it didn't matter to him whether his neighbor believed in twenty gods or no God. It mattered to Backus.

John Leland turned out to be a better protector of Baptist tradition and a better Jeffersonian than Backus. His career is especially important because it moved the story of American Baptists south of the Mason-Dixon line, where they would in the nineteenth and twentieth centuries make their greatest numerical gains. Although Leland lived most of his long life in New England, he resided in Virginia from 1776 until 1791 and fought alongside Jefferson and Madison against the Episcopal establishment. Episcopalianism in the South was more than the churchly residue of British Anglicanism. It symbolized the social dominance of the old church establishment. Episcopalians were persons of high rank. Baptists were common folk who as late as the 1760s and 1770s in Virginia and the Carolinas were being beaten, jailed, and run out of town.

Leland's position on church and state was echoed later in the South among the strictest Baptist groups—the "hard shell," "Landmark," and anti-mission Baptists who translated Baptist independence into a suspicion of all worldly activities, especially politics. Some other Baptists in Virginia were less strict. While in general terms they opposed church establishment, they accepted the assumption of many other Protestant evangelicals that government should nourish religion, by, for example, passing blue laws that protected the Sabbath and regulated morals. However, Leland would have endorsed heartily the position of James Dunn, a twentieth-century leader in the Southern Baptist Convention, who argued in 1986 that Baptists had no business lending any aid and comfort to a "happy-face 'we're number one' orgy of Americanism, with God as the national mascot." That drift in the national psyche, according to Leland, was blasphemy. He didn't like the mission boards and benevolent societies that some Baptists and other Protestants were organizing in the nineteenth century. However private, those initiatives tried to make Christian practices normative in American public life. God did not need Congress. He had authorized no man or society or government to carry out business for Him. Thus Leland was dead-set against political efforts to enact Sabbatarian legislation and to stop the delivery of Sunday mail, efforts with crucial implications that we will treat in the next chapter.

Leland's strict stand against the first parties of religious correctness in America took place in an era when many other Protestant religious leaders were very much involved in American politics, especially in the states north of the Mason-Dixon line. The voices were divided as to the wisdom of religious politics. Many clergy feared that politics was essentially immoral and that any religious initiatives seeking to influence legislation would only harm religion. William McCollom, for example, in 1852 was quite certain that "the holding of office under the present system of politics is considered prima facie evidence against a man's Christianity." Others thought that heated political campaigns chilled the life of the churches, substituting political excitement for the solace of quiet spiritual reflection. In the opinion of many ministers of the early nineteenth century, preaching the "pure unadulterated doctrines of the cross" was an activity spoiled by "harangues on national policy." The most powerful caution against church leaders' encouraging their flock to parade their religious views in political meetings was that the practice would draw politicians to church meetings like flies to honey. The hypocrisy of public officials was limitless. Everyone knew that they would beg anywhere, say anything, to get votes. Why give them the opportunity to lie about their religion? Any encouragement to fraudulent religious posturing would degrade, according to one voice, the "spiritual Church" to a "mere government machine."

And yet, as many other religious leaders noted, there were so many blights on the American landscape that cried out for moral remedies. The poor and the handicapped languished without adequate care. Men drank too much, way too much, and returned to their homes to beat their wives and their children. Prostitutes plied their trade in American cities. For many Protestant evangelicals who excitedly spread their faith through privately sponsored Bible and tract societies, the lure of a Christian political party was irresistible. Whigs and Democrats tried to deck out their presidential candidates, who by and large did not belong to churches, as Christian saints. Theodore Frelinghuysen, who was the Whig candidate for vice president in the 1844 election, was in fact a strong Protestant churchgoer and made the most of that fact. He complained of the "growing cant among us that people should be indifferent to their rulers' religious sentiments and that in politics 'Papists and Protestants are all one.' "

Horace Greeley, the American newspaper editor, who entered politics from time to time as a Whig, clearly saw the dangers of this rhetoric. For one thing, it was viciously anti-Catholic. According to Greeley, "this whole broad assertion of a 'predominant National Religion' and that Religion not the Christian but the Protestant, and not the Protestant, but such Protestant sects as the majority pronounce 'Orthodox' or 'Evangelical' is fatally at variance with the fundamental principles of our Constitution." The Order of the Star Spangled Banner, which grew into the anti-immigrant and anti-Catholic Know-Nothing movement, was one of the nastiest political eruptions in antebellum America. Led by, among others, James W. Baker, a New York Methodist and Sunday school teacher, the Know-Nothings in the 1850s made considerable political capital by attacking the Irish as a threat to American morals. Irish Catholics drank. They wasted their economic resources and refused hard work. They were not sexually pure. A defense of family values provided successful political rhetoric in Know-Nothing strongholds.

Religious political activism was put to some admirable uses in antebellum American. But it worked best when it sought to aid the downtrodden, not to attack their values. In retrospect, the most admirable work of politically active northern evangelicals was their campaigns against alcohol abuse and domestic violence, and against the institution of slavery. The Protestant evangelicals who led the crusades, however, split on the strategical questions of how religion ought to enter the political arena. One body of opinion, which included many Baptists, in effect rejected political action and resolutely refused to seek legislative remedies to correct the sins of the nation. That restraint did not make them less self-righteous in their moral condemnations of social evils. Alcohol, they said, destroyed man's spiritual instincts. Slavery corrupted the soul of both the slave and the master. To the abolitionist supporters of William Lloyd Garrison, God demanded an immediate end to the sin of slavery. But God's tools were not the tools of legislative assemblies. Although God-fearing people had to wash their hands of sin, although they had to denounce sin from public platforms, they could not force the conversion of their neighbors by passing a law. They could not force their neighbors to give up practices that those neighbors had not themselves recognized as morally wrong.

Other enemies of the great sins of slavery and public drunkenness thought differently. They argued that religious people should join with nonreligious people to seek legislation to curb the behavior of people whose acts harmed others. Excessive drinking and slavery were viewed by a growing Protestant consensus in the northern states as immoral. In these matters, many came to believe that it was right to turn their moral denunciation into political action. Wife beating and slave beating were acts of cruelty and of inhumanity. To take legislative arms against businesses and institutions that made them possible was essential.

These demands were frequently made by politicians who also led the campaign to make America a Christian republic. However, a religiously informed politics and the politics of religious correctness are, we think, distinguishable. This point is in fact crucial to the argument we are making. Religious politics need not become self-righteous. A Christian who worked for a political party pledged to abolish slavery—the Liberty party, for example—did not necessarily imagine that he was doing God's work in the same way that Christians believed that Moses had once done God's work. Although abolitionists thought modern slavery an offense to God, although they also thought it an offense to human beings who believed in Christian principles, most of them did not believe that the abolition of black slavery would make America an instrument of divine justice. Too many American Christians saw nothing wrong with slavery.

In 1845 one group of such Christians organized the Southern Baptist Convention. What prompted them to form a separate regional organization was their complaint that the antislavery feeling of northern Baptists had drawn religious people into illegitimate political activity that might one day seek to enlist God to sponsor legislation against slavery. It was an argument against the party of religious correctness. However, antebellum Southern Baptists would have stood on higher moral ground, and been truer to their heritage of church-state separation, had they conceded the injustice of slavery and insisted that Baptists ought to concentrate their prayers on a spiritual reform that would give people the wisdom not merely to end slavery but to create a just society for both white and black Americans. Alas for the nation and for the slave and freedman, Southern Baptists put their biblical minds to work in defending the South's peculiar institution, a defense they repudiated only in 1995. They may have resisted the party of God as represented by the political abolitionists. But their religious preaching helped to raise a party of secession-minded slaveholders who also claimed to do God's work. Their stand turned out to be just a competing version of politically charged religious correctness. It took Lincoln to comprehend fully the tragedy wrought by the misdirected prayers of the two religiously correct parties that split the nation.

The defeat of the Confederacy was shattering. Southern Baptists, along with most other southern religious leaders, had not known God's plan for the nation after all. The misery caused by their mistake in this matter gave them strong reasons to recover their inherited principle that politics and religion do not easily mix. In some ways they did recover the legacy, turning their attention back to the business of saving souls, a business in which they excelled. Southern Baptists in the late nineteenth century were already well on their way to becoming America's largest group of Protestants. In several instances, however, they looked to government to ban behavior they didn't like. For example, by the end of the nineteenth century, Southern Baptists leaders, really for the first time, made temperance not merely a code of conduct demanded of church members but a legislative goal to regulate everyone's moral comportment. Whatever Baptists had said about the error of using the state to coerce conscience, many of them did not believe it wrong to lobby state and local governments to end the liquor trade. Southern Baptist support also helped pass legislation against gambling and for Sunday closing.

These political initiatives did not go unchallenged among Southern Baptist leaders. As one of them said, "If civil government can specify what sins man shall not commit, then it may also specify what holy rites they shall perform." At least what seemed to some to be departures from strict Baptist principles of church-state separation involved social problems that could be debated apart from questions of a religiously dictated personal morality. Drunkenness was an issue that raised general social concerns about violence and social disorder. So was gambling. And Sunday-closing laws had been picked up by many groups concerned with the plight of wage earners. It was not necessary in these cases to turn the public policy disputes into contests between God and Satan. That happened of course. It happened frequently. Even so, the victories won in favor of restrictive legislation did not mean that Southern Baptists now believed that all actions of government were henceforth to be measured by a genuine, Jesus-certified moral yardstick.

Through the years Southern Baptists have in fact agonized more than most other religious denominations over the difficulties of finding the right way to make their religious resources serve community purposes. That is because the issue of church-state separation is so important to them. On the one hand, Southern Baptists insist that religious proselytizing and national policy-making are two different and often competing activities. On the other, they recognize that too literal an adherence to the view that religion and politics are distinct activities might seem to require people to withdraw altogether from worldly things. In American life the most world-renouncing of all religious groups who descended from Anabaptist movements are the Amish. They stick to themselves. They follow their own ways and ask nothing from strangers. They pay attention to politics only when their interests are directly threatened. And, most important, they do not expect other people to live the way they do. Southern Baptists, like almost all other American religious denominations, think that the Amish go too far in separating themselves from the world.

And with respect to a workable democratic system, they do. If all the religious people in the United States interpreted their religious responsibilities like the Amish, the nation would be in deep trouble. Refusing to join a political crusade to proclaim America a Christian nation is one thing the founders had in mind in writing the godless Constitution. However, regarding one's fellow citizens as sinners who should be ignored is an idea that is not part of our secular state. While it makes unthinkable a political party of religious correctness, it also makes any sort of nation impossible. Relatively speaking, Southern Baptist traditions have encouraged Southern Baptists to expect little from political action. Until recently the interest of many of them in politics was tepid. For that reason, some argue that what appears to be a strong effort to mobilize them as a voting bloc is a good thing. Democracy desperately needs political activism, and religious motivation is just as useful to the system as any other motivation. Indeed it is. That is also to say that the results need not be good.

Southern Baptists, of course, and any other group of people who place religion at the center of their lives cannot take part in politics and yet act politically as if their religious beliefs did not matter. People do not split their personalities in this way. Even if churches or other religiously sponsored groups never took positions on partisan political issues, the people who belong to those organizations would vote in ways that reflected their religious belief. If the past proves anything, it proves that religious affiliation can affect a voter's attitudes on a broad range of issues that seemingly have nothing to do with religion.

Yet there is a difference between a Southern Baptist who is inclined to be conservative on many social issues (after all, Baptists have never expected much of the state) and a convention of Southern Baptists who have been lobbied by Baptist leaders to vote for conservative candidates because that is what Christians who read their Bible ought to do. Politics in a secular state means that there is no Christian position on whether tax cuts are a good or a bad idea, on whether the terms of congressmen ought to be limited, and whether the capital gains tax ought to be lowered. There are ways in which Christians are influenced by their religion when they take stands on the question of abortion rights, of whether feeding the poor and homeless ought to be a government responsibility, and of whether the United States ought to support the state of Israel. But that influence leads to different conclusions. None of these conclusions represents the voice of God, not in political debate.

This point leads to some final reflections about the Southern Baptist experience. In 1985, at their annual convention in Dallas, Southern Baptists seemed to move in a direction radically at odds with their past, going far beyond the political support they had given to antidrinking and antigambling legislation. The battles waged by the 20,000 members who attended were in large part over theological disputes between fundamentalists and moderates. For example, how strictly ought Southern Baptists to interpret their general position on biblical inerrancy? The larger organizational issue was how wide a range of opinion Southern Baptists were prepared to tolerate within their ranks. With respect to elected officers the fundamentalists were prepared to tolerate none, and they won. In the convention's maneuvers and in the candidates's quest for votes, the convention was intensely political, indistinguishable from the operation of a Republican or Democratic convention. However, that fact did not by itself inject Southern Baptists into the national political arena or weaken their commitment to the separation of church and state. Despite a stray comment here and there, as when James Kennedy made that claim that the Soviet Union was the only country in the world whose constitution separated church and state, most Southern Baptists in 1985 knew where they had always taken their stand.

But were they now preparing for a break from their past? What became noticeable after 1985 was that leading fundamentalists within the Southern Baptist Convention were reaching outside of the convention to form political alliances with conservative politicians and with conservative political groups. Moral decay was the rallying cry. Pastor E. W. McCally said, "We . . . need to let the world know that any kind of lifestyle won't do. For I believe that the Bible is right. . . . The God that I serve, and the one that I preach about, made Adam and Eve and not Adam and Steve." Leaving aside the crudity of the humor, McCally was doubtlessly stating a moral position on homosexuality that many Southern Baptists accepted. What was jarring in the light of history was the willingness of fundamentalists, whose general conservatism on government social policies could be explained by their traditional fears of the state, were ready to entertain strong state action to criminalize and stigmatize homosexuals who did not belong to the Southern Baptist Convention, whose practices posed no threat to public order, and whose own religion placed faith in a God who did not reject them because of their sexual preferences. A state that can ban homosexuals solely because of their purported deviation from religiously grounded moral law and the Scriptures of a particular religious tradition, however widely that tradition is shared, can ban Jews and can ban Baptists.

The two most interesting national church figures to have emerged in the second half of twentieth-century America are both Baptists with ties to the South. Billy Graham, although he remains aloof from Baptist organizations other than his own, is the closest thing to a saint that Southern Baptists are ever likely to have. And Martin Luther King Jr., although most definitely not a member of the Southern Baptist Convention, spoke a biblical language that Southern Baptists were perhaps more trained to recognize than any other group of white American Protestants. Both Graham and King, in very different ways and with very different agendas, made their religion relevant to their politics. However, we would argue that they did so, at least most of the time, while finally recognizing the dangers of making themselves part of the party of religious correctness. Graham, for example, who in the 1950s allowed himself to endorse the stands of Cold War politicians, a decision that led him into a close alliance with Richard Nixon in the days before Watergate, had by the 1980s, and in opposition to Jerry Falwell, recognized his mistake in identifying the kingdom of God with the American way of life. Rather than endorse a union between religious fundamentalism and the political right, he warned in 1991 that the "hard right" had no interest in religion except to exploit it. A witness for Christ is intended to affect people's conscience, not to energize political sloganeering.

Our position is consistent with the greater part of what has been the Southern Baptist position on church-state separation. No religious group may legislatively dictate its conscience to other people when the only issue is that conscience's claim. If religious leaders attempt to pass legislation by arguing that it is God's will, if individuals run for office saying they do so with God's blessing, if members of a religious lobby endorse candidates for office only because they claim to be born-again Christians, they offend both American politics and the religious rules of this country set up to protect the free exercise of religion. Yet the offense is easy to give and can as easily be done by people who call themselves political liberals as by people who call themselves political conservatives. Our present-day Moral Majority and the forces of the Christian Coalition may support the election of a conservative voting bloc in Congress. However, the crusades that we will examine in the next chapter, political initiatives to end the delivery of the Sunday mail and to pass an amendment writing God into the godless Constitution, were often led by people who imagined that they were progressive reformers.

CHAPTER SEVEN

SUNDAY MAIL
AND THE CHRISTIAN
AMENDMENT

A FAVORITE BARB directed at Jefferson by his enemies had it that he was "without Sabbaths." The election of a man who spent "the Sabbath in feasting, in visiting or receiving visits, in riding abroad, but never going to church" would, according to a number of outraged clerics, make public worship "unfashionable." The basis for this charge against Jefferson rested on a single event—his attendance at a public reception in his honor given in Fredericksburg, Virginia, on a Sunday in July 1799. One contemporary remarked in bewilderment, "This fact has been trumpeted from one end of the continent to the other as an irrefragable proof of his contempt for the Christian religion and his devotion to the new religion of FRANCE."

Trivial perhaps, but the charge of violating God's fourth commandment was in some political circles a serious one. For many Americans, in fact, this was a much clearer proof of Jefferson's contempt for Christianity than the esoteric claims about his connections with rationalist French intellectuals. Many Americans then, as now, expected their public officials to respect the Sabbath as a day of rest, devoted to church attendance and family prayer. Indeed, ten years later, Americans became embroiled in a long and fierce national debate over the relationship of the federal government to the sanctity of the Sabbath, a debate that severely tested and dramatically reaffirmed the godless Constitution. From 1810 to 1830, Americans argued bitterly over whether U.S. mail would be transported on Sunday and whether post offices would be open seven days a week.

As in the constitutional ratification debates of 1787–88, at stake here was whether the national government would operate its business as a secular commercial republic committed to the separation of church and state or whether it would sponsor a Christian commonwealth where the state and spiritual ideals commingled, a vision that, as we've seen, still pervaded many of the state governments. Just as in 1787–88, so in this the second great national debate over the role of religion in national public life, the separationist ideal triumphed, and the central figure in this victory was a devout Baptist. The national government declared itself concerned with matters of this world—property rights, and a flourishing American economy—not with the spiritual salvation of souls.

The battle over Sunday mail began in the small market town of Washington, Pennsylvania, in 1809, the year Jefferson's presidency ended. Its postmaster, Hugh Wylie, followed the widespread, though unofficial, practice of sorting the mail as well as keeping his post office open on Sundays to allow churchgoers from neighboring villages to pick up mail after church. The problem was that Wylie was also an elder in Washington's Presbyterian church, and in 1809 the Pittsburgh synod of the church ruled that for such an egregious violation of the Sabbath Wylie was to be excluded from communion. When he appealed this, the Presbyterian general assembly reaffirmed the ruling and Postmaster Wylie was expelled from the church. However, during the term of postmaster general Gideon Granger, Congress in 1810 passed as federal legislation for its 2,300 post offices what until then had only been custom. The U.S. mail would be moved every day of the week, and all post offices that received mail had to be open for at least one hour each day. The twenty-year war over Sunday mail had begun.

Petitions immediately came to Congress from clergy in Philadelphia, Boston, and New York to repeal the new law. The Presbyterians took the lead, joined by Lutherans, Episcopalians, Baptists, Congregationalists, and even by William Ellery Channing, Boston's distinguished Unitarian liberal. Lyman Beecher, the prominent evangelical Congregationalist, coordinated opposition to the law, as did Jefferson's nemesis Timothy Dwight, the president of Yale. By 1815 over a hundred petitions, from churches in virtually every state, had been filed with Congress urging the repeal of the 1810 law.

Congress, the petitioners argued, had mocked "the sacred design and employments of that holy day." The legislature had made "it necessary to violate the command of God," in which case "His justice will demand that adequate punishment be initiated on our common country." Sounding much like a pronouncement of the Christian right today, a New Jersey petition summed up the opposition to Sunday mail. "Our Government is a Christian Government, a Government formed and established by Christians and therefore, bound by the Word of God, not at liberty to contravene His laws, nor to act irrespectively of the obligations we owe to Him."

Postmaster General Granger and his successor, Return J. Meigs, were less committed to the nation's post offices being opened on Sunday than to the transportation of the mail on the Sabbath. Since the petitioners, however, were unwilling to compromise by separating the two issues, postal officials zeroed in on the absolute necessity of the seven-day movement of mail. Their

arguments were worldly and practical. To suspend mail movement on Sunday would present a scheduling and coordinating
nightmare with unnecessary delays, they argued. The disruption
to the economic lifeblood of the nation would be incalculable if
fast and frequent mail movement was threatened. Public officials
needed to keep abreast of "such events as might be interesting to
the nation," and merchants had to rely on the rapid, consistent
transmission of the market information from city to city that was
provided only by mail.

When bills were drafted in Congress to repeal the law of 1810,
the postmaster general and sympathetic congressmen even trot-
ted out national security issues. A nation at war with Britain
needed the fastest possible uninterrupted communications
throughout the vast Republic. If mail delivery were suspended on
Sunday on its seven hundred routes, foreign agents, it was suggested, might outspeed the federal government with sensitive
news and dispatches. And finally, the cost issue was raised. Postmaster General Meigs warned that suspending the Sunday movement of mail would dramatically increase postal rates. Mail con-
tractors usually ran stagecoaches that carried passengers as well.
If these coaches were forced to rest on Sunday, the passengers
would seek other forms of transportation, raising postal rates.

The first battle in the war over Sunday mail ended in 1817 with
the bills to repeal the postal law of 1810 dying quiet congressional
deaths, most never even brought to a vote. The precarious international situation and the pressing need for a reliable climate for
business enterprise in the brand-new national economy made it
impossible for the opponents of Sunday mail to make any head-
way. More significantly, the easy victory freed the defenders of
Sunday mail from the need to engage in constitutional debate over
issues of church and state. This would not be the case in the
next and even more divisive fight over Sunday mail in the early
Republic.

Round two began in May 1828 in New York City with the formation of the General Union for the Promotion of the Christian Sabbath (GUPCS). The creation principally of Josiah Bissell Jr., an evangelical merchant from Rochester, New York, and Lyman Beecher, the General Union launched a new and much more massive petition campaign to Congress to repeal the Postal Act of 1810. Bissell brought new organizational support to the cause with hundreds of religiously committed merchants whom he had mobilized specifically to counter the strong commercial support for Sunday mail. Like Bissell, these zealous merchants had pledged to stop all commercial activity on Sunday. Beecher, who aspired to become the leader of a vast national reform crusade, brought new political strategies, insisting on broader efforts to mold public opinion beyond merely petitioning Congress. He had the General Union, for example, circulate over 100,000 copies of a talk he had given attacking Sunday mail, a phenomenal quantity for the time. Ending the transportation of mail on Sundays and closing the post offices were as important in reforming America for Beecher as eliminating demon rum, to which end he also helped found in those same years the American Temperance Society.

The opponents of Sunday mail adopted direct-action tactics as well. The boycott was a central strategy. To become a member of GUPCS, one had to pledge to boycott all companies that ran coaches, boats, or canal packets on Sunday. Even more dramatic actions were proposed. The agitation gave plausibility to a false claim that members of the General Union stopped a mail coach passing through Princeton one Sunday and forced the driver to stay in town until the next morning. Still, the major focus of the members of the General Union was petitioning Congress, and here they were much more successful in terms of numbers and impact than their predecessors had been a decade earlier. The call for petitions went out in December 1828; by May 1829, 467 petitions had arrived in Congress, more than in the entire seven years of the earlier protest. The number had increased to over 900 by May 1831. They came from all regions of the Republic, though mostly from Presbyterian and Congregationalist churches in the Mid-Atlantic and New England states. The typical petition contained between 20 and 50 signatures, though one from Boston had 2,000 signatures and one from New York 7,000.

A strong dose of localism and populism runs through the arguments found in the petitions. Religious issues were left in other respects to the states, it was asserted, so why not leave the full observance of the Sabbath to the states? Petitioners asked, "Can Congress, by one or two sentences in regulating her Post Office Department, virtually repeal and annul all these state laws?" Another proclaimed, "The general Government has not the constitutional power to authorize the violation of the Sabbath." The Maine Association of Congregational Churches raised the recent cry of democratic rebellion: "We will let Congress know that our rulers *shall obey us; that WE are their MASTERS!!*" But the principal theme was the familiar one used against the Constitution in the ratification debate of 1787–88. America, according to a North Carolina petition, was "a Christian Community, where all the chartered rights and political institutions, as well as the legislative provisions of the country, recognize the authority of the Christian religion." To move and deliver mail on Sunday was a sinful violation of God's will, threatening the future of the Republic. Sunday mail, petitioners from Ohio wrote, had a "direct tendency" to destroy that "piety and morality, so necessary to be cherished by a REPUBLICAN PEOPLE." A new theme that emerged in these petitions involved an ironic reversal of the arguments of 1787. Sunday mail, one petition insisted, was the "American Test Act," which, like the British Test and Corporation Acts, reserved the public positions of the Post Office for non-Sabbatarians, a religious test that violated the constitutional right of the free exercise of reason.

Some 240 petitions came to Congress between 1828 and 1831 from defenders of Sunday mail as well. These and widespread editorial opinion reiterated the commercial arguments of the previous round. Many merchants, especially those far removed from the great East Coast seaports, wrote about delays in receiving the latest information on market fluctuations. Petitioners from Trumansburg, New York, argued that Congress was required "to speed the transportation of the mails so that merchants living in different parts of the United States may have equal advantages." This theme was easily generalized into a broader theory of the purpose of government, which invoked the general liberal consensus that we have seen to have been so powerful at the founding of America. Government's concern was with worldly goods (and by extension, their speedy movement), not with otherworldly salvation. So wrote the pro-Sabbath mail editorialist "Locke" in the *Nashville Republican*. Similarly, a congressional advocate of continued Sunday mail reminded his colleagues that "the first duty of the Government is to protect its citizens in their property."

Defenders of the Sunday mail on this round took the initiative in defending the godless Constitution as the framework for the national government. Some condemned the General Union's campaign as the first stage of the "Christian party's plan" to seize control of the national government. A critic of Beecher wrote that he sought to "obtrude . . . bigotry or . . . exclusive orthodoxy into the halls of Congress." The postmaster of Perryville, New York, saw a plan afoot to "coerce and subject the mind to sectarian views," and in Poughkeepsie a large public meeting was told that Bissell and Beecher were the "entering wedge" of a "grand system" that if not stopped would produce "an ecclesiastical hierarchy" as "oppressive and dangerous" as any in history.

The legislatures of three states filed petitions with Congress in 1830 opposing repeal of the 1810 law. Indiana's included a ringing endorsement of the godless federal Constitution. Passing laws "to regulate or enforce the observance of religious duties" infringed on the freedom of religion. "Any legislative interference in matters of religion" constituted "a violation of both the letter and the spirit of the Constitution." The Indiana petition sternly concluded, in words as meaningful today as in 1830, "There are no doctrines or observances inculcated by the Christian religion which require the arm of civil power either to enforce or sustain them: we consider every connection between church and state at all times dangerous to civil and religious liberty."

What was Congress to do? The public demand to repeal the Postal Law of 1810 was much stronger this time around, eliciting, in turn, articulate and forceful defenses of the godless Constitution not found in the earlier round. One thing Congress did was to take the whole issue much more seriously than it had in 1816 and 1817. House and Senate committees devoted detailed study to the question. Samuel McKean, chairman of the House Committee on the Post Office and Post Roads and a candidate for governor in Pennsylvania, waffled. He applauded, on the one hand, the vigorous effort of those wanting to end Sunday mail. Never before, he noted, had Americans given a "stronger expression" of their preference on a public issue in terms of "the numbers, the wealth, or the intelligence of the petitioners." He was sympathetic, then, to closing the post offices on Sunday, but moving the mail was a different matter; it was too important to be stopped. Unscrupulous and speculative men of "enterprise and capital" would use private expresses, while honest traders would be disadvantaged by their lack of information.

But McKean's was not to be the decisive voice. Congress would be swayed by the chairman of the Senate Committee on the Post Office and Post Roads, General Richard M. Johnson of Kentucky, who eighteen years earlier had become a national hero as an Indian fighter in the War of 1812, the putative slayer of the great warrior Tecumseh. In his committee's report to Congress,

Johnson, a devout Baptist, delivered a thundering rebuke to all efforts to repeal the 1810 legislation. While it does mention the commercial aspects of the issue, its principal thrust is a lengthy theoretical endorsement of the godless Constitution and the strict separation of church and state. The Baptist conviction lived on; Jefferson would have been delighted.

The Senate's *Report on the Subject of Mails on the Sabbath,* produced by Johnson in January 1829 (with extensive help from his close friend Obadiah Brown, minister of Washington's First Baptist Church), is an amazing document. Too little remembered today, it stands as a landmark statement of the founding generation's Enlightenment and liberal commitment to a secular national government. Johnson framed the report around his belief that congressional action to stop Sunday mails was utterly unconstitutional, for it would establish "the principle that the Legislature was a proper tribunal to determine what are the laws of God." Were Congress to give in to the General Union's demand that the Sabbath be respected by federal law, it would exercise a power the Constitution had denied it—and, moreover, "wisely withheld" from it, for Congress was merely "a civil institution, wholly destitute of religious authority."

Johnson's Senate report did not stop there. It proceeded to lecture Congress and the nation about the place of religion in public life. It reminded Americans that they were unique. The rest of the human race "of eight hundred millions of rational human beings, is in religious bondage." But this "catastrophe of other nations furnished the framers of the Constitution a beacon of awful warning," and in their founding document they provided means to "guard against the same evil." Johnson and Brown then offer a Jeffersonian historical reading of religion that would have pleased any Enlightenment philosophe. Americans have to realize that religious leaders, seeking to incorporate their tenets with political institutions, have over time "attained great ascendancy over the minds of the people." Religious zeal, enlisting the "strongest prejudices of the human mind . . . excites the worst passions of our nature under the delusive pretext of doing God service." Vivid reminders of history's "scenes of persecution" and "the cries of the burning victim" are recounted in the report. How often, it asks, "when man undertakes to be God's avenger" does he "become a demon . . . lose every gentle feeling . . . become ferocious and unrelenting?"

As Jefferson did, the report contrasts early Christianity "in opposition to all human governments" with its perverted modern form "clothed in political power." The "meek spirit" of the former has been replaced by the "massacres and murders" of the latter. With pointed references to Bissell's and Beecher's General Union, the Senate report asks, "Did the primitive Christians ask that Government should recognize and observe their religious institutions?" America's founding fathers understood only too well this sad history and the truth represented by the early Christians. Johnson and Brown insist: "The framers of the Constitution recognized the eternal principle that man's relation with God is above human legislation and his rights of conscience unalienable."

Even in its few practical paragraphs, where the worldly issue of the mail's suspension for even one day is described as threatening the defense of the country or undermining businessmen's confidence in the honesty of markets, the report offers a lyrical hymn to Enlightenment ideals. The mails bring religious letters, newspapers, magazines, and tracts to every house in the Republic. "The advance of the human race in intelligence, in virtue and religion itself, depends, in part, upon the speed with which the knowledge of the past is disseminated." Improvements in morality and politics and in the arts of life will be confined to the neighborhood where they originate without speedy and efficient interchange between different sections of the country. "The more rapid and the more frequent this interchange, the more rapid will be the march of intellect and the progress of improvement." The philosophe meets the typically exaggerating practical politician as the Baptists Johnson and Brown plead that "the mail is the chief means by which intellectual light irradiates to the extremes of the republic. Stop it one day in seven, and you retard one seventh the improvement of our country."

Having enlisted the Enlightenment, the authors of the report turn finally to individualistic liberal theory to justify their recommendation to the Senate. To repeal the 1810 law would be to sanction by law religious opinions and observances. That is "incompatible with a republican legislature, which is purely for political and not religious purposes." Governments have no authority "to coerce the religious homage of anyone." Majorities have no authority over minorities with respect to their beliefs; they have it only in "matters which regard the conduct of man to his fellow man." In a dramatic and unusual move for 1829, one particular minority is singled out for concern by the Baptists Johnson and Brown. "The Constitution," they write, "regards the conscience of the Jew as sacred as that of the Christian, and gives no more authority to adopt a measure affecting the conscience of a solitary individual than that of a whole community." Legislators were not intended, nor did they have any power, to "define God or point out to the citizen one religious duty." The lecture concludes with the general lesson that "the line cannot be too strongly drawn between church and state." The proposed legislation violated the First Amendment, according to Johnson and Brown, clearly using what we today call its broader reading. It is obvious that no establishment of a national church was intended by the cessation of Sunday mail, yet such an action by Congress, the report's final sentence insists, is "legislating upon a religious subject and therefore unconstitutional."

General Johnson was so proud of his *Report on the Subject of*

Mails on the Sabbath that he had Congress print large numbers of it, which were then sent free to constituents, given, of course, the postal privileges of a senator. Cheap pamphlet editions were also sold around the country, and popular engravings appeared praising Johnson and his report, with the legendary Indian fighter now depicted as the heroic author of "the New Declaration of Independence" or "the Supplement to our Bill of Rights." Hezekiah Niles, the editor of the popular weekly *Niles' Register,* recommended Johnson's Senate report to his readers in order to counteract the "deluge" of "religious clamor" that the opponents of Sunday mail had raised. There were thousands in America, the editor noted, whose true understanding of the Constitution lagged far behind their "assumed acquaintance" with the "law of God." How times have changed; General Johnson did very well politically by his defense of the godless Constitution. His 1829 report and its popularity transformed his image from that of Indian fighter to that of national statesman, and in 1836 he was elected vice president of the United States, serving with Martin Van Buren until 1840.

Sunday mail ultimately fared less well, as we all know. First the railroad and then the telegraph, after 1844, changed forever the commercial climate in America, and seven-day mail service lost its most powerful economic rationale, providing up-to-date market information. By the 1850s postmaster generals were eliminating most Sunday movement of mail, and after the Civil War it slowed even more. Similarly, post offices were gradually closed on Sundays by local postmasters as the transportation of mail on Sunday ground to a halt. In 1912, almost exactly a century after their crusade had begun, the opponents of Sunday mail claimed a victory. A coalition of Protestant ministers and postal clerks finally got Congress to close for good all post offices still open on Sunday.

The story of Richard Johnson, Baptist Indian fighter and vice president of the United States, reminds us, however, that for fifty years after its founding a strong national consensus existed on the utterly secular nature of the federal government, whatever local and state law and practice may have been. His story also reveals the fundamental flaw in the Christian right's version of U.S. constitutional history. It is not true that the founders designed a Christian commonwealth, which was then eroded by secular humanists and liberals; the reverse is true. The framers erected a godless federal constitutional structure, which was then undermined as God entered first the U.S. currency in 1863, then the federal mail service in 1912, and finally the Pledge of Allegiance in 1954.

This is a good point at which to remind ourselves that the forces of religious correctness don't always enter politics with a conservative social agenda. It is the Christian right that today is seeking ways to ascribe to the Constitution a religious purpose. However, much of the support for Sabbatarian legislation in the nineteenth century came from people who thought of themselves as progressive reformers who deplored the materialistic drift of their country. They represented the upholders of an old moral economy who worried about the unfettered spirit of American capitalism. Josiah Bissell and Arthur and Lewis Tappan, leaders in the fight to stop Sunday mail delivery, were successful businessmen who deplored the common practice of merchants and manufactureres to work their employees seven days a week. Bissell and the Tappans expected to see their employees at church on Sunday and donated lavish sums of money to support their vision of a Christian commonwealth. In the political climate of pre–Civil War America, that vision acted as a radical critique of the American nation and the American way of life. People of all political persuasions have at one time or another been convinced that a good cause required the subversion of the godless Constitution.

However, the godless Constitution has persisted. It did not die with the end of Sunday mail or with any of the other compromises that have been etched into our national symbols. It won more battles, as it had in 1829. Most dramatically it fended off a concerted effort begun during the Civil War to put God and Christ directly in the Constitution through a Christian amendment, a campaign that would last deep into the twentieth century. The idea was itself not new. It had been suggested in the ratification debate, as we've seen. Jefferson's critic the Reverend Mason of New York had also complained in 1793 that "from the Constitution of the United States, it is impossible to ascertain what God we worship, or whether we own a God at all." If Americans were as irreligious as their Constitution, he feared, God might crush them and their nation to atoms. In 1811 the Reverend Samuel Austin, later president of the University of Vermont, singled out as its "one capital defect" that the Constitution "is entirely disconnected from Christianity." The leading Presbyterian clergyman in Kentucky and president of Transylvania University worried in 1815 that although the United States was "confessedly a Christian nation," nowhere in the Constitution was "God the Savior recognized." Learnedly he confided, "We could not have expected less from Plato or Cicero." It was a recurring national theme. The chaplain of the New York state legislature preached in 1820 that the founding fathers showed "a degree of ingratitude, perhaps without parallel," in drafting a Constitution "in which there is not the slightest hint of homage to the God of Heaven." By 1845, ministers began to suggest that the omission of God from the Constitution was the source of any and all American problems. The Constitution was condemned as "negatively atheistical, for no God is appealed to at all." One Protestant preacher suggested that the Constitution actually gave greater care "to the prejudices of the INFIDEL FEW, than to the consciences of the Christian millions."

The Civil War finally prompted a group of Protestant clergymen to do something about God's absence from the Constitution. The call came first from the great reform-minded Hartford theologian Horace Bushnell, in a sermon preached the Sunday after the First Battle of Bull Run. The harsh sacrifices of the war, he insisted, would be America's payment for her long spiritual indifference. Americans had lived since 1787 under a national government divorced from any religious foundation and based upon "godless theorizing." It was impossible to revere a document that failed to acknowledge that all authority was derived from God. Bushnell proposed that "it might not be amiss, at some fit time," to amend the preamble to the Constitution with a declaration of God's authority. To do so would cut off "the false theories under which we have been so fatally demoralized."

Bushnell's call was picked up by a New York City paper, the *Independent,* then considered America's most important and broad-minded religious publication. An editorial urged immediate action on his proposal as a correction to "this atheistic error in our prime conceptions of Government," from which flowed the general "atheistic habit of separating politics from religion." A chorus of clergymen joined the call. God was burying America in a ruinous war because He was ignored in America's founding document. Only if God and Christ were placed in the Constitution could His favor be regained. As the historian Morton Borden has put it, "the Civil War, so it seemed to thousands of religious Americans, was God's punishment, not only because of slavery, but because He was omitted from the Constitution."

Two separate conventions, one in Sparta, Illinois, and one in Xenia, Ohio, produced in 1863 the National Association for the Amendment of the Constitution, soon renamed the National Reform Association. Representatives from seven states were urged by the Presbyterian layman John Alexander to work for a constitutional amendment that would recognize "the rulership of Jesus Christ and the supremacy of the divine law." Others wanted wording that would pledge "faithful administration of the government according to the principles of the word of God." Alexander was elected first president of the association, and after meetings in Pittsburgh and Philadelphia the group agreed on its proposed rewording of the preamble of the Constitution:

> We, the people of the United States, humbly acknowledging Almighty God as the source of all authority and power in civil government, The Lord Jesus Christ as the Governor among the Nations, and His revealed will as of supreme authority, in order to constitute a Christian government . . . do ordain and establish this Constitution for the United States of America.

The drive for the Christian amendment quickly gathered supporters. Association committees were appointed throughout the country, and the General Assembly of the Presbyterian Church in the United States of America formally urged support for the proposed amendment. Although most of the association's members were Presbyterians and Methodists from small towns and rural areas in the Midwest, important Americans from elsewhere rallied to its banners as well. Its list of honorary vice presidents soon included one U.S. senator, two governors, three federal judges, three state school superintendents, twenty-five college and university presidents, and eleven Methodist and Episcopal bishops. U.S. Supreme Court Justice William Strong, a Presbyterian elder, succeeded Alexander as the association's president, even as he sat on the High Court bench.

Delegates from the National Reform Association visited President Lincoln in February 1864 to read him their proposed constitutional amendment and to win his support, as they put it, for "a distinct and plain recognition of the divine authority in the Constitution of the United States." Lincoln was cordial and tactful, indicating general sympathy with their religious convictions but insisting, "as the work of amending the Constitution should not be done hastily," that he needed to study the matter further. He did or said nothing about the amendment during the remaining fourteen months of his life.

There was, of course, fierce opposition to the amendment. Seventh-Day Adventists saw it as a frightening threat to religious freedom. Isaac Leeser, the Jewish editor of the Philadelphia newspaper the *Occident,* mobilized Unitarians, Deists, Jews, and Catholics against the amendment. Pressure from "Hebrew friends" in Massachusetts seemed to have turned its distinguished senator Charles Sumner, originally a supporter, against the amendment. When a petition arrived in Congress claiming that God was "baptizing the nation in blood" as punishment for a "Christian nation with an atheistical Constitution," the board of delegates of American Israelites offered a counterpetition. "This omission of a creed has not been hurtful to Christianity any more than to Judaism," it responded. How could the petitioners believe America was cursed by God "because He has not been recognized in the Constitution?" Has he not given America "eighty years of prosperity, blessed it on land and sea, in its basket and kneading trough, in field and city?"

Important constitutional objections were raised as well. Newspapers accused the National Reform Association of a "deliberate intention to abridge the history of conscience in America." If it succeeded in putting Christ in the Constitution, "a Jew or an infidel would be outside the Constitution." Some saw the amendment's meddling with the Constitution as the "first step taken in the formation of a State Church." Another observer noted in 1868, in explaining his opposition to adding religious clauses to the Constitution, how it was "exceedingly strange that as the old world is struggling out of the tyranny and corruption of an alliance of the church with the state, we should be struggling to set the same yoke upon our necks." And then there is Horace Greeley's wonderfully American dismissal of the National Reform Association. "Almighty God," he wrote, "is not the source of authority and power in our government; the people of The United States are."

Congress was no more responsive to the Christian amendment than Lincoln was. In 1864 it simply ignored the National Reform Association's petitions and addresses. In 1869 an Illinois petition to the Senate "praying for an Amendment to The Constitution of The United States, recognizing the obligations of The Christian religion," found not a single senator to support it. The proposed amendment did make it to the committee stage in 1874, however, while the sitting Supreme Court justice Strong was president of the National Reform Association. To no avail, for the House Judiciary Committee decisively reported unfavorably on it. But the association would not give up. With a dogged persistence it hung on at the periphery of American public life until 1945, unsuccessfully launching major campaigns in 1894 and 1910 to put Christ into the Constitution.

The eighty-two-year crusade waged by the National Reform Association to save America with a Christian amendment was picked up by the National Association of Evangelicals in 1945. Twice, in 1947 and 1954, it staged unsuccessful campaigns to add to the Constitution the words "This nation divinely recognizes the authority and law of Jesus Christ, Savior and Ruler of Nations, through whom are bestowed the blessings of Almighty God." In these crusades, efforts to adopt a Christian amendment were invested with distinctly conservative political implications.

However, in recent years the Christian right, unsuccessful in attempts to change the godless Constitution, has totally reversed its strategy. In a staggering historical flip-flop, it now celebrates that Constitution by denying its godless foundation, which so many religious leaders in the past clearly recognized and lamented. Having lost many times in its efforts to put God and

Christ into the persistently vilified godless Constitution and an atheistic national government, the Christian right today embraces the Constitution and its authors, rewriting history as it does so. Its adherents have falsely dressed the founders of American government and the Constitution in godly Christian garb, which, they argue, later godless generations have systematically torn off. America today will suffer God's wrath, we are now told, unless it returns to its founders' abiding vision of a Christian American politics. Such is the vast distortion of American history offered by today's preachers of religious correctness. We must turn next to the Christian right's prescriptions for politics today, better informed as we now are of its erroneous reading of America's past.

CHAPTER EIGHT

RELIGIOUS POLITICS AND AMERICA'S MORAL DILEMMAS

MORALITY AND VIRTUE are not issues that belong exclusively to the religious right or, for that matter, to religion. They concern everyone interested in the future of democratic society. Some of the founders of this nation were Christian; others were not. Many of them were members of churches; many others were not. What they shared was a view that religion should not divide people, an opinion that provided them with sufficient reason to exclude God-based claims from most sorts of political debate. On the other hand, their desire for a nondivisive religious climate stemmed directly from their belief that religion was an indispensable civic resource. If the American people could not maintain moral standards in their public and private dealings, they could not make democracy work. A people without compassion or mercy, a people without a sense that social injustices suffered by their neighbors were social wounds to the entire commonwealth, a people without honesty or integrity, a people without the capacity to forgive and to sacrifice, a people who refused to care about the effect of their self-interested actions upon others, above all, a people who could not safeguard the hopefulness and idealism of its youth—such a people would surely perish from the earth, having prepared no future generation to mourn them.

Despite, or rather because of, this passionate concern for morality, the founding fathers made no constitutional provisions for the national government to instruct its citizens in matters of moral and religious conscience. They did not want America to be godless, only its government. How, then, did they imagine that a democratic state could ensure that its citizens would incorporate moral codes into private conscience? The simple answer is that they did not. A democratic government was not created to produce moral citizens. It was the other way around: moral citizens constructed and preserved democracy. The founders left the business of teaching morality to private concerns, a principle that should carry some weight with present-day conservatives. It follows from this formulation that if the United States at the end of the twentieth century has lost its moral way, many of our voluntary institutions, including our megachurches and our television ministries, have badly let us down.

Indeed they may have. But responsibility for moral problems is never easy to assign. We may take some comfort in recognizing that there never was a golden age of moral behavior in the American past. Pick any point in the history of the Republic. Read the journals, newspaper editorials, and public addresses of the time. The depressing news about moral decay was as sensational then as it is now. Anyone who wishes to ignore these diatribes from not so long ago and insist that things, morally speaking, *were* better in the nineteenth century ought to note, with respect to the question of why our ancestors were our moral superiors, that churches were not as well attended then as they are now. Neither were the public schools in those halcyon days when McGuffey's Readers purportedly took care of the moral and religious instruction of the nation's children. However, trying to excuse ourselves by making flattering comparisons with the past is as nonproductive as imagining that there was once a golden age. Any nation with our current levels of violent assaults, drug-related murders and suicides, teenage pregnancies, child abuse, AIDS, and white-collar crimes had best concentrate on the present realities.

But, whatever our plight, we must never forget the many good reasons why the founders did not look to politicians and the state to inculcate morality. Our first presidents and legislators looked upon politics, as we understand that activity today, as a corrupting activity. Although Jefferson, called an atheist by the religious right of his time, believed fervently in the social importance of religion as the foundation of morality, he did not confuse the work of government with the work of churches and private citizens. As leaders of the religious right now correctly state, Jefferson insisted that government do nothing to interfere with the moral work of private agencies. What those leaders have stated less correctly is that his caveat that government not discourage religious work also placed upon government an obligation not to encourage it—not, in any case, in a way that privileged it over the work of nongovernmental secular agencies.

For Jefferson the moral possibilities of democracy depended on keeping America an agricultural nation. That is, he did not think that democracy and the morality necessary to sustain democracy could flourish under social conditions that destroyed the economic independence of individuals. When the United States, after Jefferson's death, committed its future to the industrial revolution, when it encouraged the growth of large cities and of gigantic economic institutions that hardened class lines in America, public morality encountered problems that it had not known before. That fact was clearly recognized by people of all political persuasions. Too many of the rich did not need morality. Too many of the poor could not afford it. The burden of sustaining public morality fell heavily on the already overburdened middle classes, and disproportionately on middle-class women, who, curiously, were told to stay at home and not interest their pretty heads in the corrupting business of politics.

Simply put, we live in a world where we cannot assume that moral behavior has universal appeal, regardless of what we teach. In fact, we are constantly discouraged by the reality that the people who should be our solid citizens, the people who know the moral rules and who by dint of all manner of privileges are in the best position to live by them, fall regularly into corrupt practices involving money, power, and sex. There is plenty to worry about and only limited help to be gotten from the founding fathers, who were nagged by their own particular problems of public morality and who could not have foreseen the special problems that hover over society at the end of the twentieth century. Nonetheless, the attitudes of the Enlightenment that shaped the course of the American Revolution have not lost their relevance. As we have argued throughout this book, the founders of this nation would regard the mixing of religion and politics in the ways now being engineered by the religious right as part of the problem of failing public morality, rather than as an answer.

We have indicated along the way that Pat Robertson is an excellent example of how the religious right has misread the intentions that lay behind the Constitution and of the dangers contained in that misreading. His case merits extended attention. A religious leader turned politician, Robertson ran for president in 1988, hoping to turn his appeal as an avuncular talk show host who has built a media empire into charisma on the hustings. In 1988 that didn't work. However, through the Christian Coalition, which he created, Robertson has effectively raised money for conservative candidates, provided an army of volunteer workers for politicians who share his views, and emerged as a powerful figure in the Republican party.

What is the message? Robertson's books and speeches decry the country's moral decline and blame the decline on the enemies of religion. He has a long and a short view of when this moral rot set in. The long view rests on a loopy conspiracy theory involving Freemasons and Illuminati who wandered through the eighteenth century stirring people up against kings and clerics. The story has been around a long time, and in most history departments, including in all likelihood the one at Robertson's own Regent University, it has been thoroughly discredited.

In Robertson's short view, America's moral decline started with a cabal of New Deal liberals, a category of secular cosmopolitans whose number just happened to include a lot of Jews who ran banks but liked Karl Marx. These secularists hated the Christian religion and have since the New Deal wormed their way into positions of power with the explicit intention of wiping out religious faith. Two seconds of reflection ought to convince anyone that this bizarre scenario has no credible basis in fact. But Robertson knows, and herein lies one of the dangers, that when people are worried, imagined enemies can take on supernatural abilities. Once liberals can be turned into agents of Satan, then Robertson doesn't have to supply them with plausible motives or explain how they can so cleverly fool well-meaning people.

Robertson's comments about the New Deal never once let on that the country was in the midst of the worst depression in its history—that men and women with families could not find work, that people were standing in line for food, that individuals were having their religious faith severely tested because their children were sick and hungry and because churches had run out of resources. The Americans who voted for the New Deal were not dupes. They formed, in fact, a political constituency that was heavily churched. Robertson's unfounded charges against liberals who hate God and moral decency is an inexcusably careless reading of the American past. As a misuse of religion to advance a political agenda, it constitutes exactly the sort of corruption that the founders feared when ambitious men rose up and announced that God had chosen them to found a political movement. It is the sort of thing that gives populism a bad name.

The people with the best reason to attack Pat Robertson are devout Christians who care about the credibility of their faith. They object to the partisan uses he has sought to make of the passion of Christ. There are many versions of Christianity. But not one of them worthy of respect, and especially not the Pentecostal faith where Robertson began, would trivialize the agony and suffering of its redemptive God into campaign slogans for politicians. Faith, to be blunt, is irrelevant to many of the political causes that Robertson has forcefully championed. Not to all of them, and we shall come to those issues. What needs emphasis now is the fact that Robertson's self-declared war to save the soul of America is not with secular humanists, as he says. It is with other Christians.

In truth, it is sometimes hard to make out just who counts as a Christian in Robertson's view of the world. On the one hand, Robertson is quite certain that America is a Christian nation and that its Christianity explains its greatness. For example, he contends that the United States has succeeded because "those men and women who founded the land made a solemn covenant that they would be the people of God and that this would be a Christian nation." Shoring up this argument, Robertson variously estimates that 90 percent of the American people are Christian and that almost 50 percent of them regularly attend church. Although there is room to quarrel with those figures, the general point that Robertson means to make is fair enough. Compared with most Europeans nations, America boasts a high proportion of citizens who state that they believe in God, that religion is important in their lives, and that they identify in general terms with a Christian faith as opposed to any of its rivals, including atheism.

Yet Robertson fails to follow up the implications of what he has written about moral decline. If Americans are Christian—in fact, if they are by dint of church membership more Christian than they were a hundred years ago, and vastly more Christian than they were in the eighteenth century—then how do we explain the decline of religiously based morality? Can it really be that a cabal of God-hating liberals has succeeded, despite the overwhelming numbers confronting them, in driving religion from the public square? And without anyone's suspecting, before Robertson and other leaders of the religious right came along, what they were up to? An alternative theory might suggest that too many religious leaders have stopped doing what they do well and started doing what they do badly, in alliance with men who don't care much about religion at all except when it returns votes.

We thus have an anomaly. If moral decline is evidenced by the rate of divorce, the amount of extramarital sex, and the increase of abortions, all part of the record cited by Robertson, then clearly the 90 percent of Americans whom Robertson cites to prove that the United States is a Christian nation are deeply implicated in the decline. Why, then, does Robertson, as a religious leader, not turn his gaze on the Christian churches of America, and the kind of gospel message they preach, and look for problems that might exist there? For the most part, Robertson is uninterested in the strengths or the failures of organized religion, or the possibility that religion may be its own worst enemy. The villain for spiritual decline is the state, which never in this country carried the burden for maintaining the spiritual health of the people or for teaching them how to pray. Roger Williams would have smelled a rat. If religion isn't making people who profess to believe in it good, neither can the Republican or the Democratic party.

Nonetheless, many religious Americans have been touched by claims made by the religious right that government is not neutral in religious and moral matters. They have been mobilized by calls to take some sort of cooperative political action to reverse what they perceive as liberal-led measures that abrogate a long-standing moral consensus about values, especially ones that touch on sexual behavior. The consequences in the political arena have been impressive. A number of smart pundits have suggested that in the midterm elections of 1994 that swept conservative Republicans into control of both houses of Congress, the Christian Coalition established itself as the single most powerful voting bloc in the nation.

If that is so, it is in no small measure due to the skills of Ralph Reed, a man with a Ph.D. in American history and an innocent youthful appearance that masks what is probably the shrewdest political mind in the religious right movement. Pat Robertson tapped Reed to give the Christian Coalition a less contentious aura. Most especially, Reed has labored, without deleting the word "Christian" from the name of the organization and its journal, to free the organization of its deserved reputation for anti-Semitism, bathroom humor directed at women in public office, and purveyance of sleazy political gossip.

The Christian Coalition, under Reed, ostentatiously welcomes Jewish members who share its value concerns. It publicly rejects the view of one Southern Baptist minister tied to conservative politics that God does not hear the prayers of Jews. In his own bailiwick Jerry Falwell seems to have gotten at least this point and has insisted that the Moral Majority imposes no religious test. He has stated, "I would feel comfortable voting for a Jew or a Catholic or an atheist as long as he or she agrees with us on the vital issues." After the United States, the greatest nation in the world, says Falwell, is Israel. That pronouncement rests on a quirky base, that is, the conversion of Israel to Christianity prior to the battle of Armageddon. Nonetheless, it explains why the Moral Majority and the Christian Coalition have been defended by the editors of the Jewish New York journal *Commentary*. In addition, many Catholics who were the primary victims of Protestant political movements in the nineteenth century have endorsed the Christian Coalition.

Since Falwell and others have repeatedly insisted that America was founded on the Christian faith, one must wonder about the consistency of the message that the Christian Coalition promulgates. But Reed seems determined, if not to take Christ out of the Christian Coalition, at least to move him to one side. It might be possible to do that. The authors note with gratitude that many of the people who use the facilities of the Young Men's Christian Association in Ithaca, New York, where they regularly play racquetball, are neither Christian nor male. The name of the YMCA is historic, meaningful to some, less meaningful to others. The important thing is that it does not get in the way of anyone who wishes to use and to support a resource that does, after all, make an important contribution to the moral life of the community. The strength of great religious traditions in the United States, we can all agree, should be a source of pride in American life, not a cause for embarrassment. However, a great religious tradition is not always served well by those who speak for it.

Reed is a born-again fundamentalist Christian, but he is a born political junkie with a specific but a flexible political agenda. What he has announced as the Christian Coalition's legislative proposals for a "Contract with the American Family" is an endorsement of the broad economic goals of conservative Republicans. Wrapping the secular and the moral up together, Reed uses the label "family values" to accomplish two things of practical political importance. It implies that those who oppose the package aren't loyal to their spouses and don't love their children. It also allows the Christian Coalition plenty of room to be pragmatic. If restrictions on abortion rights won't fly, then attack welfare spending. If prayer in the school doesn't appeal to enough conservative voters, then argue that increased spending for the military is Christian. If you sense that no one will vote for legislation to make divorce more difficult, and certainly not leading Republican men, then link high taxes to moral decline.

Religious fundamentalists are not necessarily happy with this sort of politics. Many of them suspect that Ralph Reed's leadership of the Christian Coalition has let the organization become the tool of the conservative wing of a Republican party that has no burning interest in its moral agenda. They are also suspicious of Reed's "stealth" tactics, in which Christian candidates are encouraged to play down a moral agenda while running for office. A moral purpose that has to disguise itself appears to them to be a poor way to change people's hearts and minds. Our view is that the fundamentalists are right in holding these suspicions. If so, it won't be the first time in American history that religious leaders with a moral political agenda will learn that big-league politicians who covet the Oval Office want power first and treat everything after that as negotiable, depending on prevailing political winds.

Reed does not intend to be anyone's patsy. He means to turn the Christian Coalition into something more formidable than the Sabbatarian organizations of the nineteenth century, the groups that up to this point the Christian right has most closely resembled. Sabbatarians imagined their enemy to be a party of secularists who wanted to destroy churches, tear down Sunday schools, and abolish the "Lord's Day" by delivering the mail on Sundays. Their political efforts fizzled because they were finally interested only in a single moral point. Reed is determined to avoid that weakness. His fundamental ambition, which he states candidly, is to take over the Republican party and, in effect, to create something that has always existed in many European nations but never in the United States—a religious or confessional political party.

Religious parties do not mark the end of freedom, as experience in many European states has indicated. That is because the religious aims quickly get submerged by secular issues that any ruling party needs to address if it is to stay in power. Yet a religious party seems distinctly out of place in a country that made the elimination of an established church one of the first orders of national business. Reed has repeatedly denied a number of charges leveled against the Christian Coalition—that it seeks to make Christianity the official religion of the United States, that it seeks to cram its moral values down the throats of other unwilling Americans, that it has contempt for people who are secular. That has been difficult, not because he doesn't believe in the broad base he wants to build for his political movement, but because many members of the Christian Coalition don't.

One model of religious politics that Reed frequently invokes is the civil rights movement led by Martin Luther King. King's genius, Reed correctly notes, was to tailor a religious message that could reach a largely secular culture. In Reed's mind, the sort of religious politics that propelled the civil rights movement can be used to create an analogous sort of religious politics to drive a pro-family movement. His analogy isn't persuasive. Reed certainly understands what made King effective. King's message called for healing and reconciliation: "Our aim must never be to defeat or humiliate the white man but to win his friendship and understanding. We must come to see that the end we seek is a society at peace with itself, a society that can live with its conscience, that will be a day not of the white man, not of the black man, that will be the day of man as man." King's dream of a society cleansed of racial injustice was an inclusive vision that called upon all Americans to share in a mission of simple justice.

Inclusion. That is what defeats Reed. If ever he can come up with a way to write a pro-family speech, one that will be acceptable to the Christian Coalition, that calls upon gays and straights, feminists and Christian fundamentalists, atheists and Roman Catholics, unmarried welfare mothers and Pat Robertson to join hands and sing the words of the great spiritual "Free at last, Free at last, Thank God almighty, we are free at last," he will have done something that might yet move this nation. But that isn't the message he is even remotely close to delivering. The Christian Coalition is a political movement with too many sour voices in it, whose use of religion has divided and stigmatized people.

To be sure, Reed makes a good point against many of his critics when he notes that religious leaders on the left have often in American history promoted a liberal agenda of government relief programs for the poor and powerless. The Social Gospel of the left has more than once drawn up specific policy recommendations concerning pending legislation on such matters as child labor, minimum wage, and fair labor practices. The temptation to become a political lobbying group runs along the spectrum of religious politics. So does the temptation to morally stigmatize your opponents. The classic example in American history is the case of religious abolitionists who made slavery an issue of sin. Surely slavery was a great moral evil. Yet when those on the religious right suggest that you can't condemn the Christian Coalition without condemning the abolitionists or the liberal-oriented political action committees of the National Council of Churches, they almost have a point.

It isn't a direct score, because it ignores an important difference between the Social Gospel of Christians who have used the ethical teachings of Jesus to warn against class and racial injustice and their own version of applied Christianity that too often seems to be merely an apology for wealth. The Social Gospel movement at the end of the nineteenth century and during the first part of the twentieth argued that the moral teachings of the Bible put the case for the weak against the powerful. Christ spoke for the poor and defenseless and cast moral blame not on those who suffered but on those who could not be moved by their suffering.

Most of us are not about to go out and sell our property and give it to the poor. Human beings aren't ready to be that good, at either end of the social scale. On the other hand, if people can't be touched by the call of compassion that is central to the New Testament, if the comforts of privilege are so great that the religious contribution to public debate becomes an invitation to ignore the poor and the homeless, then religion has nothing distinctive to say. It becomes just another sad sign of the times that the country may have lost a conscience to reach, that no one wants to hear a political message, whether religious or secular, that makes people uncomfortable. The difference between King's moral plea for racial justice and too much of the Christian pro-family program of everlasting patriarchy is the difference between the voice of the religious prophet who calls upon an unjust society, for all societies are unjust, to transcend itself and the voice of ecclesiastical judges who have a particular set of sins with which to charge heretics. Granted, it isn't always easy to tell the difference, but with respect to any important effect that religion can have in the American public sphere, the difference matters.

Pat Buchanan's is another voice on the Christian right worth reckoning with, although one somewhat different from Reed's and especially Robertson's. For one thing, monied power doesn't impress him. His sense of right and wrong arises from the American Catholic ghetto of Washington, prior to Vatican II, and the strictness of the parochial schools, whose teaching staff of nuns were not averse to corporal punishment. Furthermore, Buchanan is not shy about blaming churches for their failure to uphold standards. Buchanan's respect for government started dropping with the administration of John Kennedy. His regard for his church plummeted even faster during the contemporaneous papacy of Pope John XXIII. When you get right down to it, Buchanan's problem with the United States is that the Catholic Church let itself be swallowed whole by Protestants who had never truly believed in families, not big families where mothers and fathers in their own separate ways exerted iron discipline. His famous call for a religious war at the 1992 Republican National Convention, a bit of political rhetoric that sounded like something out of the Crusades and did George Bush a world of harm, is best understood as a cry for his own church to get off its duff.

Yet, for all its populist resonance, Buchanan's religious voice offers the same unwise mixture of religion and politics that we have criticized throughout this book. In the past, it was almost always Protestants who crossed the line between church and state in inappropriate ways, and almost always Catholics who pointed it out. There is no little irony in that fact given the way that Protestant ministers attacked John Kennedy in 1960. But Buchanan sometimes appears to have let himself be transformed into a Protestant Sabbatarian whom his forebears detested. His position is not consistent. At times he speaks with the voice of a classic libertarian—stay off my property and I'll stay off yours. This is the voice he uses to turn back the argument that the nation as a whole owes special consideration to any group because of past and present discrimination. For example: "To us, sin is personal, not collective; it is a matter for personal confession, personal contrition, personal reconciliation with God. . . . We have no sense of guilt of Wounded Knee; because we weren't at Wounded Knee."

With respect to religion and politics, what is interesting in the above statement is that Buchanan is really endorsing the position of John Locke. The statement is also a rejection of any notion of the United States as a covenanted nation—a doctrine that maintains that if America tolerates a great sin, whether or not an individual ever has been in any way directly complicit in that sin, God will punish the nation as a whole. Some such notion has usually informed religious politics in the United States. Some Christian abolitionists, including the militant William Lloyd Garrison, put slavery in that category of sin. Many members of the Christian Coalition regard abortion in that light.

Buchanan, when he takes this straight libertarian position, may seem to be at odds with his own church, which in the full conservative majesty of its pre–Vatican II voice, proclaimed the reality of original sin, that is, the collective stain of guilt visited upon humankind because of what Adam and Eve did. Buchanan was not at Eden either. But Buchanan also has another voice that takes over his political rhetoric when he confronts what he regards as an immoral practice. Then he asserts, "Whose moral code says we may interfere with a man's right to be a practicing bigot [presumably an interference Buchanan accepts when actual harm can be demonstrated] but must respect and protect his right to be a practicing sodomite?" Confronted with open homosexuality and feminism, Buchanan joins the proponents of a theocratic state: "The Old and New Testaments are not only infallible guides to personal salvation; they contain the prescriptions for just laws and the good society—for building a city set upon a hill." Since Christians cannot agree about what the Bible says, indeed have never agreed, this statement cannot be taken seriously even on its own terms.

Perhaps that is the heart of the offense to American politics presented by politicians who claim to know what God wants. People who belong to America's major religious traditions hold different views on social policies, and wherever there is something approaching a moral consensus it is one shared by all people of good will. You don't have to be a theist to condemn murder and to love your children. And to be a Christian does not commit you to the view that abortion is murder and that Hillary Clinton is a bitch. The religious right, especially as it grows powerful and cannot credibly cast itself as a beleaguered group of outsiders, runs the grave risk of creating opposition to organized Christianity not because of its brave stands taken to defend the oppressed of the earth but because of its pragmatic crusades to protect the self-interest of the white middle class. The white middle class has plenty of means to defend its political interests. It does not need the churches to act as its political lobby.

Potentially, the most powerful card in Ralph Reed's deck is his ability to recruit African Americans who are sick and tired of seeing their neighborhoods torn apart by violent crime, drug abuse, and careless, very careless, sex. But we have yet to see how skillfully the Christian Coalition and its Republican allies will play this card. It is reasonable to argue that there is a moral breakdown in America's inner cities. But it is not reasonable, and certainly not wise, to promote religious remedies as a government panacea. The result is to divert debate away from hard policy issues toward virtually meaningless initiatives that constitute symbolic politics and nothing more.

The furor over school prayer is a good case in point. If anything is unconstitutional, it is government encouragement to pray in the public schools. Moreover, the proposed constitutional amendment to allow voluntary prayer is offensive on two counts. First, it violates explicitly the intended secular base of the Constitution. And far worse, it encourages the political use of religion in a way that allows elected officials to evade their real responsibilities and to claim for themselves a moral high ground that they too often have done nothing to earn. Is it any wonder that many politicians love to talk about school prayer just as they like to talk about flag desecration? School prayer is a perfect example of symbolic politics. To propose it can arouse loud cheering, but it will solve not one of the social problems of the ghetto, and most especially not the problem of guns in the schools.

If we cannot as a society teach our children virtue without bending our government to sponsor religiously vapid prayers as a way of saying "in your face" to some evil group of secular humanists, then we are caught in a kind of trouble that lies beyond the remedy of government and our elected officials. That would surely be the substance of Thomas Jefferson's answer to Newt

Gingrich, who misquotes and misrepresents Jefferson's line "I have sworn upon the altar of almighty ["almighty" is not in the Jefferson phrase] God eternal hostility against every form of tyranny over the mind of man" to justify a school prayer amendment. What Jefferson said in private was about his private beliefs. And it was directed precisely at efforts by religious leaders to implicate government in the sponsoring of a religious practice. That effort was the tyranny.

On the other hand, we hasten to add that we find absurd the policy adopted by many school districts in the United States that effectively bans the discussion or mere mention of religion in the school curriculum. Such policies constitute a serious misreading of Supreme Court decisions and give legitimate cause for complaint not merely to religious fundamentalists but to anyone who cares about the academic content of courses in history and literature. In our opinion President Clinton erred while governor of Arkansas in securing legislation to institute a moment of silence in the schools, because that moment was clearly intended as a prayer surrogate. Nonetheless, his speech in July 1995 declaring that the First Amendment "does not convert our schools into religion-free zones" was mostly on target. The constitutional ban is against school-sponsored religious worship and religious indoctrination, not against scholarly instruction that makes clear just how important religion has been in shaping not only American culture but the culture of peoples around the world.

Nor is religion restricted to academic lessons. Students may pray to themselves if their prayers are not disruptive and do not interfere with their attention to instruction. Outside of class but still within the school building, they may argue about religion with their classmates, just as they might argue about any other subject. A religious club may publicize its meetings like other school clubs. This is simply to say that in appropriate extracurricular settings and at appropriate times, the religious practices and ideas of students have the same right to circulate and be talked about as any other set of ideas and practices. President Clinton tried to establish some general guidelines because he knew that school districts fear lawsuits. That is a problem in our litigious society. Nonetheless, the wiser heads in Washington in both political parties have recognized that a constitutional amendment proposed by some members of the religious right to permit what is already permitted—that is, private prayer by individuals in public places and the inclusion of academic study of religion in the school curriculum—is unnecessary. It only implies that government has restrictive powers that were never given to it.

In arguing the case for the godless Constitution, we have treated people associated with the Christian Coalition as principal opponents. However, as we shall see below, what is conventionally labeled the religious right is not the sole contemporary manifestation of religious correctness. Godless politics was not invented by the framers to create a godless America. Quite the contrary. However, the concept, as we have tried to show, has created considerable nervousness through the course of American history among people who are thoughtful and intelligent. Many people disagreed with Thomas Jefferson in his own day, and many people disagree with him now. It might clarify the debate if we recognized that we are not all his children. James Bryce, the English visitor to the United States in the late nineteenth century, whose *American Commonwealth* is something of a classic, aptly characterized the attitude of many Americans:

> The matter may be summed up by saying that Christianity is in fact understood to be, though not the legally established religion, yet the national religion. So far from thinking their commonwealth godless, the Americans conceive that the religious character of a government consists in nothing but the religious belief of the individual citizens, and the conformity of their conduct to that be-

lief. They deem the general acceptance of Christianity to be one of the main sources of their national prosperity, and their nation a special object of Divine favour.

That is not what Jefferson meant by a wall of separation between church and state.

Bryce claimed too much, but his observation made plain that neither the "no religious test" clause of the Constitution nor the First Amendment settled the issue of church and state in the United States. Rather than full consensus, we had in the past, and we have today, an ongoing debate. We would be foolish to suggest that there is a fully consistent way to implement the position we defend, and any position with respect to the question of religion and politics in the United States should remain supple and negotiable. Two things, however, our case will not compromise. First, while the godless Constitution does not exclude religion from the public square, it insists that religion can claim no special privileges. God does not attend political conventions in America. Second, the "godless politics" dictated by the "no religious test" clause means that a person's religious faith, or lack thereof, should never be an issue in partisan politics.

Americans don't like to imagine that the old corrupt countries of Europe are somehow doing better than theirs is. This seems to be especially true of France, which to many has been corrupting American virtue since the days of Thomas Jefferson and Benjamin Franklin. Still, France understands the meaning of "no religious test." It has elected presidents in the twentieth century who are atheists and who are Jews and has done so without a great deal of fuss. It is very difficult to imagine this happening in the United States in the near future. This country, which abandoned an established church first, has kept an informal test for its highest office the longest. We need only remember how long it took for many Americans to believe that a Catholic could be trusted in the White House. And we have had only one of those.

To some, of course, the observation about France only recon-firms their worst fears about godless nations. France, along with Holland and Sweden, has gone to the dogs, say many American religious leaders, because of secular humanism. Holland doesn't outlaw cannibis and permits euthanasia. France promotes sex and all other forms of sensual pleasure. Sweden runs a welfare state that drives people to suicide. None of these countries expects government to act as moral policemen over private behavior, and none boasts a very high level of religious observance. Compared with the United States, they have extremely high taxes. Nonethe-less, with respect to most of the social issues having a moral di-mension that bedevil the United States today, such as crime in the streets, deadbeat fathers, or unwed teenage mothers, they all are in much better shape than the United States. Our suggestion has been that part of our problem is that we don't use religion as a resource in the way it was intended. We allow our politicians to render it banal, even to turn it into a blinder that diverts our at-tention from hard issues.

Can we, then, marshal the resources of religion in the political arena in ways that do not violate the fundamental principles of a secular state and that do not tear the country apart along confes-sional lines? Yes, but it depends on how that marshaling is done. Religion in the United States is organized by groups of private in-dividuals. In that sense, a religious body in America is not differ-ent from the Heritage Foundation, the American Civil Liberties Union, or the Benevolent Order of Elks. Religious leaders are free to say whatever they like in this country and to enter politics if they like. There are very few religious actions in politics that are unconstitutional. There are simply religious actions that are wise and unwise, generous and ungenerous, informed and uninformed. Wearing a clerical garment to a political meeting is perfectly legal, but it doesn't guarantee you respect or give you the right to go to the head of a long line of speakers.

Some calm and intelligent persons, however, will not be persuaded by our argument and will still insist that religion is a special case. It is special, they say, because the founders recognized its importance to morality and because most Americans are influenced by political issues that seem to touch on their religious faith. The distinguished American sociologist Robert Bellah has suggested that Americans possess, without anyone's conscious design, a consensus-building civil religion. Although originally derived from Protestant Christianity, it preaches no dogma of any one theology. Although it borrowed freely from the imagery of the Bible, and especially from the story of Exodus, it is clearly differentiated from any of America's churches. Citing the rhetoric of a number of American presidents, Bellah located the heart of this civil religion in the "American tradition, namely the obligation, both collective and individual, to carry out God's will on earth."

Bellah announced this national creed, which is at bottom an ecumenical version of covenant theology, during the bitter days of American involvement in Vietnam. The last thing he wanted was to encourage a national hubris, a sense that whatever the nation did must be what God wanted. The high priest of Bellah's civil religion was Abraham Lincoln, who wondered constantly about what God might expect of him but never imagined that he really knew. Lincoln's famous second inaugural address, taken seriously, was a confession that the nation, in asking its young men to sacrifice their lives in battle, might hope that it was doing something consistent with divine justice, yet might in fact be doing something much more ambiguous. The North and the South could not both be right in claiming divine favor. Lincoln called upon religion to keep himself and the side that he led humble.

If Bellah had been a historian rather than a sociologist, he might have recognized that the civil religion he invoked was more often used in the political arena to stir a sense of national arrogance than to make the nation realize how risky it was to claim God's blessing for national policy. Lincoln was the exception. Jimmy Carter was the last American president whose religion reminded him in a serious way of what the nation was doing wrong and had been doing wrong for a long time. Carter believed that that is what a religious perspective is supposed to provide a national leader. He learned, however, and he made the point for Ronald Reagan, who did not need to be taught, that the religious politics of guilt and doubt has very little voter appeal.

Bellah apparently believed that there might be a happy medium. He approvingly quoted the language of Lyndon Johnson, who in signing the Civil Rights Bill of 1965 referred to the Latin motto on the great seal of the United States: "God has favored our undertaking." Johnson continued, "God will not favor everything that we do. . . . I cannot help but believe that He truly understands and that He really favors the undertaking that we begin here tonight." Civil rights was a good cause, but if God thought anything on that day, it was surely about how long the United States had deferred doing anything to further this good cause. Considering what Johnson was about to do in Vietnam, and how many references he made to God to justify that war, we would do well to regard Johnson as a cautionary example.

Civil religion, in the hands of our presidents, rarely serves American political debate. That is especially true because many Americans are too inclined to believe that the United States has some special place in God's scheme. It's fine to think that God has written the rights of men and women into the laws of nature. Jefferson did believe that. However, when politicians use God to rally voters around their favorite partisan issues, they corrupt the principles that Jefferson wrote into the Declaration of Independence. If the authors of this book could with tongue in cheek promote a constitutional amendment to shore up national morality, it would not be one to protect the flag but one to state that any elected official who so much as hints that he or she is doing God's will can be impeached. The quickest way to make religion serve the public causes it is intended to serve is to make sure that it can't grease the way for those seeking political office.

Senator Phil Gramm's shameless advances to the Christian right provide an especially vivid example of what we condemn. In campaign speeches and mass-mailed letters, Gramm paraded a belief in Christ's Second Coming to win votes. Quite aside from the issue of the sincerity of his beliefs, which in the political arena is always suspect, Gramm ostentatiously violated the Jeffersonian view that politicians, in deference to the "no religious test" clause, should keep their religious opinions to themselves.

We cannot follow the counsel of Richard John Neuhaus, who calls the notion that America is a secular society a dangerous doctrine. Neuhaus is no friend of the religious right, partly because of his distaste for its theology (Neuhaus is a Lutheran turned Roman Catholic) and partly because he sees too much anti-intellectualism in the movement. Nonetheless, Neuhaus argues that the religious right taps a deep discontent in the United States—a discontent that arises from "the denial of the obvious" fact that the United States is "in some significant sense . . . a Christian people." Neuhaus can quote many authorities, including some older decisions of the Supreme Court, that affirm the Christian base of America.

Yet just who is denying this fact, which is obvious to him and whose obviousness is imputed to others? If American society is composed largely of Christian people, then Neuhaus and the others who are comfortable with that perception have little to worry about. His concern about a public square that is naked of religious influence is unfounded. The "secular" Supreme Court, it is true, has banned prayer in the public schools along with Bible reading; it has made it difficult to display religious symbols on public property; and it has not relaxed in any significant way the nineteenth-century ban on aid to parochial schools.

Compared, however, to what the founding fathers did when they cut churches off from tax support, these restrictions are in fact secondary. With the important exception of aid to church-run schools, most of them have made little difference to anyone. The truth of the historical matter is that religion is far more evident in public life today than it was at any time during the nineteenth century. That is only in part because the media have made everything more visible in public life. George Washington didn't light a Christmas tree in Washington. The first Congress didn't have to deal with the legions of religious lobbies that now do business in the nation's capital. The tax authorities of the nation didn't need to devise policies for church-run businesses. The Supreme Court didn't have to consider possible violations of the establishment clause, because the issue didn't come up. Cases arise now not because religion has been marginalized but because it is ubiquitous. It floods the airwaves of the nation, radio and television, largely because the Federal Communications Commission stopped trying to use its authority to promote religion. That is, it stopped forcing the networks to give away time for religious programming. The free market, in this case as in most cases, vastly increased the opportunity for religious opinion to find an audience.

Whether this public presence of religion has increased the spiritual resources of Americans is another question, one with, in our opinion, a far from reassuring answer. However, the government of the United States, when it acts in a secular way as it is supposed to act, does not harm religion. Nor does it harm democracy. Contrary to what Neuhaus writes, the drafters of the Constitution believed that people could support democratic institutions without believing that those institutions were God directed. Need we add that many leaders around the world cite a divine blessing for actions that destroy democratic institutions? We cannot say too often that it is people who found and maintain political institutions, not God, and that it is people who must take the praise or the blame for what they decide to do.

According to Neuhaus, political conflicts cannot be resolved without a transcendent or religious point of reference. With all due respect, that is nonsense. Religion is a great help in reminding everyone that democracies rest on the principle of imperfection, an imperfection that requires compromise and bargaining among constituent groups that hold different views about what is the good life. The process of democracy is surely, at its best, a moral process. Yet the founders created the Constitution of this very good land precisely because they recognized that if we as a people knew what truth was, and what God wanted us to do, we would not need politics or democratic government at all. Moreover, although many of them were Christian, and all of them admired the moral lessons of Christ, they did not believe that Christianity was the only source of sound morals. When they talked about government and politics, they showed far more mastery of the classical authors of Greece and Rome, who formed the core curriculum of America's colonial colleges despite the religious affiliations of those colleges, than of biblical texts.

Religious correctness heralds a contrary set of propositions. It refuses to recognize secularism as a fundamental principle of American government. It asks that we perpetuate in public rhetoric the notion that the United States is an instrument of divine providence. It objects any time values other than its version of Bible-based Christian values are accorded status in public policy decisions that government is trying to destroy religion. Religious correctness, in this respect, either doesn't understand the principle of government neutrality toward people's moral and religious convictions or doesn't believe in it. It fears that if the American people are not as Christian as they used to be, it must be the fault of public policy decisions that seek to reinforce Jefferson's wall of separation between church and state.

Government policies surely have an effect on social morality. That point scarcely needs to be argued. It is a fair complaint, and one that has been made with sophistication by Stephen Carter, who teaches law at Yale, that religion, because of our concern to prevent government sponsorship of religion, can be unfairly hobbled in open public discussion. That complaint was recently recognized by the Supreme Court when in a controversial decision it held that if a public university chooses to subsidize the publication of a range of student journals that express a wide variety of opinions, it cannot refuse such support to a religious journal. That is not to say that a theist has a right to demand that the University of Virginia hire a Creationist as a member of its biology department. But, as Carter demonstrates in *The Culture of Disbelief,* the "fairness" question gives us much to argue about.

It is also legitimate to ask questions about the moral effects of almost any government policy—even a proposal to cut taxes. It is a fair argument against a proposed policy to say that it undercuts stable families, that it loosens sanctions against the careless sexual behavior of single teenage parents, boys and girls, or that it is not tough on crime. Again we agree with Stephen Carter that it is wrong to ridicule persons who professes to hold a political position because it is required by their understanding of God's will.

However, an argument in the political arena is merely that, a point of view that may be challenged by other points of view that reflect a different morality or a different prediction about the moral consequences of government policy. It is not legitimate for political leaders to mobilize religion in order to invest their argument about moral consequences with certainty, to imagine that their understanding of God's will should be shared by everyone. We have repeatedly claimed that politicians who run for office claiming God's backing and who urge voters to make their decisions on the basis of a candidate's religious beliefs are treading on ground that the Constitution did not want entered. On this matter we do not agree with Stephen Carter, who is offended "by suggestions that our politicians are wrong to discuss their views of God, or that members of the clergy have no business backing what candidates they will, or that voters should never choose among candidates based upon their religious beliefs." That is precisely our set of suggestions, which people in this free country are free to ignore but which we think work to the advantage of both politics and religion.

How, then, can we handle the most pressing political issues of our day that involve serious differences about religious and moral values? What about abortion? We believe that in a democratic society abortion advocates and abortion foes can legitimately and passionately debate the issue in the political arenas where public policy is crafted, be they legislative, administrative, or judicial. In these debates moral and religious convictions will and should play a prominent part. What is unacceptable to us in light of the godless Constitution is for religious certainty ever to trump politics and for government policy in any way to privilege or codify religious belief in ways that preempt a pluralist democratic process. Public policies in the United States must never be put to a litmus test of religious correctness. To do so fundamentally violates American tradition. It was just such religious tyranny that the framers of the Constitution feared and why they drafted a secular document that made the operation of government indifferent to religion.

What is moral? To pass out condoms in the classroom? Or to permit an inexperienced parent without resources to try to rear a child? Many Christians and non-Christians won't show much enthusiasm for either option. But as people argue about what to do in these cases, both sides will be wrestling with moral issues that cannot be cleanly settled one way or the other. That makes for good, albeit agonizing, debate and for healthy politics. It allows for religiously informed perspectives to be heard but in a manner that raises those perspectives above the level of idle or coercive God talk.

Whether religion in the future will remain a vast cultural resource, one that will allow us to advance with compassion and with the courage to imagine that we have not yet explored the full range of what it means to be human, depends not upon government but upon whether religious leaders in this country are smart enough not to confuse what they do with what politicians do. Otherwise they may win some political victories only to discover that political victories are meant to be the most transient phenomena in the life of a democratic republic. The framers of the Constitution knew perfectly well their predecessors' beliefs about the necessity of enforcing religious orthodoxy to preserve social peace. But they committed themselves and the United States to another option—one that recognized that social peace and personal happiness are better served by separating religious correctness from public policy. The success of what they proposed should still fill us with amazement and with gratitude.

CHAPTER NINE

GEORGE W. BUSH
AND THE
WALL OF SEPARATION

SELDOM HAS THE wall of separation between church and state seemed so fragile as in the America of George Walker Bush. While some references in the original chapters of our book are dated—Ralph Reed no longer heads the Christian Coalition, for example—the concerns we raised about what he and others represented are stronger now than when we first wrote the book. The religious politics of Ronald Reagan and George Herbert Bush look statesmanlike when compared to the tactics used by the incumbent administration headed by George W. Bush. As a result, we are a deeply divided nation. If the election of 2004 made anything clear, it was that unhappy and sobering reality. In a dangerous world where bipartisanship is desperately needed in order to work to minimize the threat of biological and nuclear terrorism, the United States is caught in a domestic war where bipartisanship has almost disappeared as a political reality. Perhaps not since the Civil War have the country and the national government been so polarized.

However, this time the division is not defined by the Mason-

Dixon line. More than any other factor, the country is divided along religious lines, the type of faith or lack of faith that puts many decent, honest Americans in defensive postures and sets them against many other decent, honest Americans. Who would have imagined, given the origins of this country, that at the beginning of the twentieth-first century Americans would split angrily along lines about what political party best represents the will of God? White evangelical Protestant Christians have been pinpointed as a primary cause of this polarization, but the vast majority of them are not responsible for what has happened. As we have argued throughout this book, when religion becomes divisive in the public sphere the only winners are politicians. Their short-sighted gains take a terrible toll on our democracy and our collective moral resources.

How did we come to this point, and so quickly? In the presidential campaign of 1960 the Democratic presidential hopeful John F. Kennedy spoke to a group of conservative ministers in Houston, Texas. Some of those ministers were stalwart figures within the Southern Baptist Convention. Their fear was that Kennedy, a Roman Catholic, could not behave in office independently of obligations placed on him by his Church. Among the concerns of the pastors gathered in Houston and of other Protestants across the nation, not all of them conservative, was whether President Kennedy would move to appoint an ambassador to the Vatican, or seek government funding of Catholic schools, or try to legislate Catholic teachings on birth control and divorce. Among other things Kennedy said, "I believe in an America where the separation of church and state is absolute—where no Catholic prelate would tell the President (should he be Catholic) how to act, and no Protestant minister would tell his parishioners for whom to vote . . . and where no man is denied public office merely because his religion differs from the President who might appoint him or the people who might elect him." Kennedy pledged to be a president whose decisions were not conditioned by any "religious oath, ritual or obligation," a president who did not speak for his Church on public matters.

Although the Protestant ministers in Houston remained skeptical, no one ever accused Kennedy during his brutally truncated term as president of having violated his pledge, of acting in any way to give currency to the charges once leveled against him. The election of 1960 seemed to mark a watershed in American history when all Americans, of whatever religion, had pledged allegiance to church-state separation.

A decade later that consensus remained intact. In *Lemon v. Kurtzman*, a landmark case that reached the Supreme Court in 1971, less than a generation ago, an almost unanimous court ruled against allowing salary subsidies to parochial, almost entirely Roman Catholic, schools for the teaching of certain "secular" subjects. That court, made up of Justices Burger, Black, Douglas, Harlan, Stewart, Marshall, Blackmun, Brennan, and White, defined an era when judicial decisions concerning the religious clause of the First Amendment, whatever the split, went forward under a consensus that "separation of church and state" was the proper way to interpret the phrase "Congress shall make no law respecting an establishment of religion." The famous *Lemon* test enunciated three guidelines to judge the constitutionality of any law passed that affected religion: The statute had to have a secular purpose. Its principal effect could not be to advance or inhibit religion. And it could not "foster an excessive government entanglement with religion."

Chief Justice Warren Burger, a Nixon appointee to the Supreme Court, rested his decision in part on his concern, one also enunciated by the founders, about the intrusion of religious issues into political debate. His decision is worth quoting at some length:

> Ordinarily political debate and division, however vigorous or even partisan, are normal and healthy manifestations

of our democratic system of government, but political division along religious lines was one of the principal evils
against which the First Amendment was intended to protect.
The potential divisiveness of such conflict is a threat to nor-
mal political process. . . . We have an expanding array of vex-
ing issues, local and national, domestic and international, to
debate and divide on. It conflicts with our whole history and
tradition to permit questions of the Religion Clauses to
assume such importance in our legislatures and in our elections that they could divert attention from the myriad issues
and problems that confront every level of government.

It has been the primary argument of this book that Chief Justice Burger got it right. Religion has strong potential to divide people, for good as well as bad reasons. Given the emotional force
generated by religion, sensible public policy demands an effort
to minimize the consequences of religious division in shaping
public policy. In 1971 Burger was reiterating a consensus that
most conservative religious groups shared with other Americans.

Something has happened to destroy that consensus. Thirty
years later in the presidency of George W. Bush, *USA Today*
reports that only half of Americans believe that "maintaining the
separation of Church and State is important." Already, the con-
tested election of 2000 had illustrated the new reality. God did
very well, indeed, in 2000. The public square reverberated with
talk about God, as if only believers could be good presidents—
and as if presidents were chosen to be defenders of the faith, not
defenders of the Constitution. In his first campaign for the presidency, George W. Bush consistently performed on the stump as
someone who had proclaimed over the years that "my faith tells
me that the acceptance of Jesus Christ as my savior is my salvation and I believe that." He no longer said, to be sure, what he
had said in 1993, that people who did not accept Jesus Christ as

their personal savior could not go to heaven, since many who were excluded from heaven could vote. Still, he boasted of reading the Bible daily. When asked what thinker had most influenced his life, he said Jesus.

In 2000 Democrats worked to catch up in the contest to keep God alive and well in their party. Al Gore, a Southern Baptist like his predecessor Bill Clinton, looked stiffer than he usually did when he let everyone know, more than once, that he was a born-again Christian and that whenever he faced a tough decision he asked himself WWJD, What Would Jesus Do. Perhaps attending multi-million-dollar soft-money galas in Hollywood did not count as a tough decision. Gore had little choice. Pollsters who told him that he was in electoral trouble with religious America forced his turn toward Jesus. What else could he do when he learned that 40 percent of Americans thought that the Republican Party "shared America's fundamental faith in God," whereas only 18 percent said the Democrats did? What indeed would Jesus do to get rid of the trail of Monica Lewinsky?

Enter Joe Lieberman. As the *New York Times* columnist William Safire put it—in the best journalist's one liner of that campaign—it took a Jewish Hail Mary pass to keep the Democrats in the game. Yet in Gore's choice of Lieberman, the key factor was not his Jewishness, but his unassailable, unembarrassed religiosity. In his debut appearance on August 8, 2000, with Gore in Nashville, Lieberman mentioned God 13 times in 90 seconds. One hopes the Guinness Record people were nearby. This was surely a record. As forcefully as the Christian Right, Lieberman worked to quiet American nervousness about the lack of religion in our politics. This was a shame.

But what truly undermined the 1960–70 consensus on church and state was the success of George W. Bush. All presidents have a personal narrative that shapes the public's perception of their character, from Lincoln's log cabin to Jack Kennedy's *PT109*,

Clinton's man from Hope, and George Bush the elder's transformation from New England patrician to Texas entrepreneur. George the younger is the first president to make religious conversion his defining life story. Like the confessional genre's inventor, St. Augustine, Bush renounced a dissolute early life of debauchery by accepting God, in the modern case through the intervention of Billy Graham in a 1985 walk along the Atlantic Ocean in Maine. Bush puts his post-conversion relationship with God at the center of who he is and what he does in private and in public. Thus he told Bob Woodward, in recounting his decision to invade Iraq, that "going into this period I was praying for strength to do the Lord's will. . . . I'm surely not going to justify the war based upon God. . . . Nevertheless, in my case, I pray to be as good a messenger of his will as possible." With a president who so deliberately blurs spiritual and secular categories, is there any wonder that public commitment to church-state separation has declined? While John Kennedy had to convince America and its Protestant majority that he would keep his distance from religion, never mentioning prayer as his guide in the Cuban Missile Crisis, the convert's zeal of Bush requires would-be twenty-first-century presidents to convince many religious Americans that they are, in fact, candidates of faith, whose faith will shape what they do in office.

In the election campaign of 2004, President George W. Bush, some kind of Protestant who courts conservative evangelicals, took the stand of pro-life, a coded term signifying his wish to use his office to limit stem-cell research and to weaken a woman's right to have an abortion. John Kerry, a Roman Catholic, took an opposite position and, although he spoke a good bit about his faith, took the same stand on church-state separation as John Kennedy, declaring that a Catholic president is not the servant of his Church. Important clergy in his Church, however, were bolder than they had been in 1960, despite the pedophile scandals that had in recent years rocked the Catholic Church. Archbishop Charles J. Chaput of Denver said just before the election that Catholic voters who pulled the lever for abortion-rights candidates, like Kerry, would be committing a sin that must be confessed before receiving communion. What is astonishing is that this spectacular interference in an American election by a Catholic prelate, a view that was voiced by other American Catholic archbishops and bishops, caused not a ripple of protest or outrage from conservative Protestant evangelical groups.

Nor did many conservative Protestants seem angered by the metaphorically violent threat of evangelical leader James C. Dobson that his flock of one million members of Focus on the Family would put six Democratic senators "in the bull's eye" if they continued to block Republican conservative judicial appointments. Clearly, the separation of church and state has lost an important part of its Protestant constituency.

The Republican victory in November 2004, albeit by the narrowest margin given to any incumbent president who was reelected, seems to have made religious converts across the spectrum of professional politicians. Worried Democrats gathered in urgent sessions to talk about how to fit the party more comfortably with the purported religious passions of most Americans. Carl Rove wannabes started selling to the Democratic party the wisdom of finding candidates who would strike voters, especially Christian voters, as people of deep religious conviction. Secularism, they were convinced, had become a bad word, almost as bad as liberalism. Democrats discovered James Wallis, the most prominent figure on the evangelical left, and invited him to party strategy conferences. They even listened to Republicans who advised Democrats to learn how to say the word "God" and not flinch.

There was a happier time in American politics when most people and the newspapers they read would have paid little attention to these gestures. What in the world does God have to do with political calculations? Does the claim that America is a religious nation boil down to a national wish to make God a spiritual surrogate for Boss Tweed? Many conservative evangelical leaders have recognized the dangers that political opportunism poses to faith. But perhaps too many of them have been seduced by the power of White House dinner invitations. They need to speak up.

Actually, what the Democratic party and the Republican party need to get is not religion but moral passion—the sort of moral passion both parties have used in the past to evoke concern for American citizens least able to care for themselves. Lip service to Jesus, as part of a campaign stump speech, does not qualify as moral passion. Why have liberal political leaders suddenly lost a grip on the notion that those who speak for stem-cell research, for a woman's right to choose, for protection of the environment, for a national system of health care, are talking about, among other things, moral values? Why has all morality, with the backing of some conservative religious voices, been subsumed under the cause of an ownership society, embryos, and restrictive sexual attitudes that have nothing to do with the considered, not the careless, choices that most Americans make during their lives? Why, indeed, give the moral-values edge to the current Republican administration at all, to those, who, as Barbara Ehrenreich has noted, brought us Abu Ghraib. Caring for the poor, opposition to war, and truth-telling, she adds, are moral issues taught in the New Testament and the sacred texts of other world religions that have distressingly few champions in recent American political contests.

Politicians need moral passion to lead a nation. But their moral passion must address the dilemmas that human beings face in trying to improve our collective life. Morality in the political realm should never mistake itself for the voice of God. Moral passion by itself does not settle an issue, though it can give importance to what is at stake. Often political leaders and voters must confront cruel moral choices, for moral passion usually matters most when difficult issues are at stake. It is divisive enough without the insertion of someone's claim to religious certainty. The foundation principle of a democratic society is that no one person, no group of people, no political party, and no religion can ever be certain about what is the right thing to do in trying to construct and preserve a just society. World religions, all of them, teach us that human beings have many more reasons to be humble than to be arrogant. Why then is that lesson so easily forgotten by religious and secular people alike?

An important question set before liberals and progressives regarding church-state separation is about what issues undermining Jefferson's wall they should challenge and what issues they should leave alone. We can begin with the political tactics used most successfully by Republicans in the 2004 election. Do Americans who voted against George Bush and who deplored the apparent importance in the election of religiously coded value issues, such as gay marriage, have any solid gripe about an important matter of church-state separation? Or did the angry complaints they made during and after the election about the role of religion in the campaign merely reflect the anguish of sore losers?

To the extent that their objections revolved around the willingness of religious Americans to speak their mind about the issues and to cite their religion as a reason to vote for a particular candidate, the complaints are without merit. Religious identification has since the first days of the party system in the United States been a strong indicator of how people vote. White Protestants have for a long time been voting more for Republican candidates than for Democratic candidates. If faith-based judgment leads to policy proposals that strike liberal voters as wrong, it is the policy and the morality of the policy, not the faith, that needs to be attacked. If liberals think that some religious voices deflect debate away from public issues of vital importance, issues that government can do something about, to issues beyond the reach of government even if they mattered, then they need to find ways to speak passionately about what are important issues, not join the chorus saying that only religion guarantees moral sincerity. The answer to faith-based judgment is not more profession of faith in public debate, but clear-headed analysis of crucial issues touched, in appropriate cases, with moral passion.

We repeat what we said in the first chapter to our book: overzealousness in protecting Jefferson's metaphorical wall of separation is both bad politics and unwise social policy. That said, however, some things about the election of 2004 properly raise concern. One of them was the encouragement given to ministers to make political endorsements from their pulpits. The Bush folk courted ministers who endorsed Bush and concentrated a lot of attention on large congregations gathered in so-called mega-churches, churches with attendance figures soaring over 2,000. Mostly Protestant, these churches are an important part of the religion landscape in many key swing states where most of the presidential election was fought. However, Kerry, let it not be forgotten, sought and received pulpit endorsements from African American ministers. Few politicians in close elections are inclined to stand by principle if they stand to gain votes from whatever source.

The objection to pulpit endorsement of political candidates needs careful statement. The many defenders of the practice ask on what grounds anyone can challenge the free speech of ministers. Why should clerics not be allowed to say what they like from the pulpit? They can of course, although there is a possible sanction from the Internal Revenue Service. If the IRS determines that a church organization has departed from its sacred function and become an agency of partisan politics, it can, in theory, lose its tax exemption. But that is usually not the issue. Churches with ministers who speak openly about their political preferences still, for the most part, do the sorts of things usually associated with all American organized religion. That includes compiling impressive records in promoting charitable giving. So, again, on what grounds can we challenge preachers who use their free speech to make political endorsements to their congregations? Or pastors who lead their congregation in prayer, beseeching God to make sure that the right people show up at the polls and keep the rest at home?

All sides in these debates agree that free speech protects ministers who voice their political opinion in a non-church forum. Ministers as citizens ought to have political opinions. However, the issue changes when they use their opinion to sway members of a tax-exempt religious organization. For perspective, let us imagine that the president of a prestigious Ivy League university (another tax-exempt organization)—an institution that in much of the public imagination harbors a godless and liberal faculty—told a public assembly of students during the campaign season of 2004 that they should vote for John Kerry because of his support for stem-cell research. Moreover, let us further imagine that the university president proposed using a small portion of unrestricted endowment funds to pour into the coffers of Democratic candidates. In our minds, such action would justly provoke howls of protest from students, faculty, alums, and the public. What needs to be argued in this case is that universities, like churches, are not tax-exempt institutions because they are universities or churches. They receive relief from taxes because they provide something deemed important to the entire community and do it for reasons other than profit. When they divert the money they receive to the purpose of partisan electioneering, they no longer merit the tax break.

As a First Amendment right, Ivy League university presidents and ministers can say whatever they want. Moreover, as leaders of institutions that are supposed to serve the public, they can plead for social policies that in their minds create a more just and equal society. But they should not attach those policies to particular candidates for office or divert funds of the institutions they lead to electioneering or efforts to turn out voters of the right sort. When they use their office to embroil universities and churches in partisan politics, the issue is no longer about their personal free speech. It is about the misuse of their authority.

One question that needs pondering is how in the world the label "secular" acquired negative connotations. The founders of the republic, whether they were pious or generally indifferent about church going, agreed on language creating a secular state. What then has made citizens afraid of acting as secular public servants? Do most voters really believe that such people cannot have moral values or care deeply about moral issues? Do they believe that only people who claim to be religious are gifted with moral insight? If this is the common view, it needs to be challenged, and sharply challenged. In his 2000 campaign for the vice presidency, Lieberman suggested many times that only a religious people can be a moral people. If only a religious people can be a moral people, one wonders why less-religious Europeans take better care of their poor, their children, and the elderly and provide a higher percentage of their budgets to repairing the social fabric than Americans.

Unquestionably, religions, and not just Christianity, are a classic and important source of moral values. Saying that does not mean that the moral values ascribed to one religion or another cannot be challenged. Saying that also does not overlook the fact that religious groups, including Christian groups, have very different ideas about what moral values apply to questions of social policy. Not all Christians, not even most Christians, for example, object to stem-cell research. Whatever moral dangers attach to conducting research with embryos has to be matched by the moral transgressions entailed by refusing to attend to the suffering of adults, our sons, daughters, parents, and grandparents who might be helped by that research. Surely in this most powerful of nations our public leaders can brave the protests coming from certain ideological quarters of the so-called Christian Right and remind the American people of how much it owes to the work of scientists, not merely to what they have discovered but also in thinking about the moral implications of scientific work. Put another way, if the United States wants to remain in the forefront of nations, it cannot afford to leave unchallenged a notion that belief in the Virgin Birth necessarily leads to greater moral wisdom than belief in Darwinian evolution.

In the public rhetoric that shapes our contemporary collective life, nothing is more dangerous than an insistence on the moral incompatibility between a religious view of life and a secular view of life. The founders lived in the late eighteenth century when almost everyone in society professed religious beliefs. That is no longer true. Polls tell us that most Americans believe in God. Nonetheless many Americans who occupy positions of leadership are un-churched and do not look to religious authorities for moral guidance. If in fact we imagine that the only morality is religiously based morality, we are in a lot of trouble. The men who wrote the Constitution generally agreed that what made religion effective in creating moral citizens was the teaching that moral people went to heaven and bad people went to hell. That view was indeed a powerful way to enforce moral norms. But in the over two hundred years since the Constitution was written, visions of hellfire are a lot weaker than they once were. We have got to find better rewards for public virtue than the promise of heaven. Morality must grow from our recognition of responsibilities toward the "continuous human community," our obligations not just to our children and grandchildren but also to human beings who will stand on this earth one hundred years from now.

We need then to view our moral language as common property, not as something that belongs to people of a particular religion or to people of no religion. Our state is a secular one, which renders moral debate in the public sphere as something different from a theological inquiry into the nature of God's will. At the same time, self-styled secularists should never imagine that they have nothing to learn from people of faith or that the moral passion of evangelical Christians never speaks to issues that concern them. They should think about the implications of statistics suggesting that Americans who live in red states give more to charitable causes than people who live in blue states. Whatever their differences, moral Americans have communal responsibilities toward people who suffer from poverty and disease and ignorance. It is hard to decide what is the worst effect of overly partisan politics. But surely its demonstrated ability to destroy any social utility we might gain from honestly posing moral questions is at the top of the list.

Since we hold that religious divisiveness is bad for democratic politics, let us return to our caution about overzealousness in defending Jefferson's wall. We ask what contemporary issues of church-state separation should concern us and what issues are best left alone? In our opinion perhaps the most important issue has to do with the controversy swirling around public financing of faith-based charities, a policy pursued with much fanfare by the Bush administration. While all politicians have trouble viewing religion as anything more than a strategy for winning, the subject of government support for faith-based charities merits serious attention. In this area Democrats have a real opportunity to flex their faith muscles in a constructive way. Anyone who can demonstrate that faith-based charities, with government aid, can help the poor or the homeless or the addicted in our society—people without hope—deserves a hearing. The same can be said of anyone with good evidence that religious schools can help children in inner cities better than the usual public schools.

The first thing to say is that government support for faith-based charities is neither new nor in an important sense controversial. Various umbrella groups, including Catholic Charities, Lutheran Social Services, and Jewish Federations, have received public dollars numbering in the billions. President Bill Clinton supported bills known as Charitable Choice that allowed federal funds under specified grant programs to flow to faith-based organizations. These bills included sensible rules to protect church-state separation. In providing assistance with federal funds, faith-based organizations cannot discriminate among their clients on the basis of their religion or lack of religion. They cannot direct the funding to religious activities such as worship, sectarian instruction, and proselytization. The programs are judged by how well they fulfilled the secular purpose for which they received the grant. At the same time reasonable accommodation is made to allow faith-based organizations to maintain their religious identification. They do not have to strike the word Christian or Jewish from their names. They do not have to remove religious art and symbols from the space where they provide their charitable services. And they retain the right, within certain limits, to take religion into account in hiring personnel.

John DiIulio, who tried unsuccessfully to take the politics out of the faith program of the Bush White House, draws a useful distinction between faith-based and faith-saturated programs. The latter programs, which insist that proselytization and worship are essential to the good they do, go beyond what the Constitution permits. To fund their work is to set off an unseemly scramble for federal money among religious groups seeking to expand their membership and their financial resources. Whether such programs do or do not perform the claimed miracles of rehabilitation is beside the point. We must distinguish them from the faith-based and secular programs that pose no challenge to the First Amendment. In making room for government aid to non-proselytizing religious programs to get people off drugs and out of prison, we need not believe that they work better than social programs that have no connection to religion. The evidence suggests that well-run religious and well-run secular programs work equally well. Thus it is enough to follow the sensible suggestion that faith-based programs are an important resource that we should not neglect. In solving the problems of the poor, the homeless, and the hopeless, government needs all the resources it can muster. The old notion that any hint of religion in a social program compromises it beyond constitutional repair is no longer tenable.

To this point, however, the Bush administration has made a mess of its faith-based initiative, turning it into a cover to push the agenda of its most conservative evangelical supporters, including James Dobson's Focus on the Family. Observers note that little faith-based initiative money has reached non-Christian religious organizations. Pat Robertson has received a three-year faith-based grant for $1.5 million. Chuck Colson's workplace reentry program for ex-offenders, a program "saturated" with faith, has received $22.5 million. The Metro-Atlanta Youth for Christ, eager as they put it to "reach the young people of metro-Atlanta with the Gospel of Jesus Christ," has received $455,000. Millions go to Christian right organizations like Crisis Pregnancy Centers, which counsel young women not to have abortions. Bush's faith-based initiatives also extend a welcoming hand to selected African American clergy in order to increase Republican votes among black Americans.

As a result of the political strategies that lie just beneath official White House policy, the faith-based initiative has not gone very far and remains tainted with the stigma of political opportunism. If Democratic leaders seize the "faith-based" idea simply to close the "God gap" in the public perception of their platform, they will fail both to establish a sensible program and to win political support. Nonetheless, an opportunity exists because a sensible program of government support to faith-based organizations is a good idea that can command bipartisan support. As a partisan issue it will simply be an insult to faith and a socially useless program.

Quite different from faith-based initiatives that can have tangible public benefits, joining religious and secular moral goals, is the swirling controversy about the display of the Ten Commandments in public schools and in government buildings. At this moment, with the matter about to reach the Supreme Court, lower court rulings support the ban, and Judge Moore of Alabama lost his judicial seat when he refused to remove a concrete block inscribed with an abbreviated version of the Ten Commandments from the state's Supreme Court Building. In our mind the action against Judge Moore was appropriate. The Ten Commandments are not, contrary to what some people say who clearly have not read them recently, the basis of our law and only in the most general way speak to commonly held moral codes.

The first four of the commandments are specific to the religion of ancient Israel, and are not observed in their entirety today by many American Jews or by most American Christians. The Lord God who delivered the Jews from their bondage in Egypt is historically, philosophically, and theologically different from the Trinitarian God worshipped by Christians. The majority of religious Americans have no particular problem with graven images; and they do a lot of work on the Sabbath as a weekend visit to any American shopping mall suggests. As for the other six commandments, the admonitions to honor parents, not to kill or steal or lie about one's neighbors pass as moral in just about anyone's book. The ones about not committing adultery or not coveting a neighbor's wife or manservant or maidservant may seem to support family values, but perhaps do not form the best sort of instruction for grade-school children who might actually read what is posted on the wall. In any case, if discussions turn to sexual behavior, someone is surely going to point out that a greater moral menace to our society than adultery or coveting manservants is the practice of unsafe sex.

People argue that the Ten Commandments have great symbolic and historic value for school children even if not every point is particularly germane to their growth into moral citizens. The argument taken to the Supreme Court by the American Center for Law and Justice, a law firm established by Pat Robertson, is that the Ten Commandments are "uniquely symbolic of law." In fact, symbols aside, any argument that the Decalogue is the source of American law is deeply flawed. More important as a source of American law than the Ten Commandments is the English Common Law tradition and its codification in Blackstone's *Commentaries*, which contain no reference to Moses. Just like the framers, the early judges who forged the American legal tradition were more likely to cite Enlightenment writers like Locke and Montesquieu than the Torah. If we were serious about the Old Testament as the source of law, then there are a great number of specific "anathemas" in Leviticus and Numbers that we need to get serious about after centuries of neglect.

Of course the phrase "symbolic of law," in a curious homage to secularism, is meant to invest the Ten Commandments with secular rather than religious meaning. But the argument does not satisfy the Constitution. The symbolic and historic value of the Ten Commandments, their symbolic value as law, relates to a specific religious tradition. It treats that tradition as the best tradition, symbolically placing Americans who do not share that tradition in a lower rank of citizenship. The Ten Commandments do not belong in public buildings, unless they are part of a display of other historically valuable codes of moral conduct. Moses, pictured alongside Solon and Hammurabi and Mohammed, becomes a useful lesson in history rather than the display of normative religion unacceptable to many who are now Americans.

For Americans who call themselves liberal, an equally difficult issue, at least with respect to the short-term political fallout, relates to the current dispute about the "under God" phrase in the Pledge of Allegiance. God was put into the pledge in 1954, forever changing Francis Bellamy's 1892 pledge, which for the Christian socialist minister was a secular, egalitarian vision of America with "liberty and justice for all," not just for the rich. The Knights of Columbus, Reverend Billy Graham, President Eisenhower, and the U.S. Congress argued that America would triumph against the Cold War threat of "godless atheistic communism" only if it were "under God." Half a century later, many Americans regard God in the Pledge of Allegiance as what protects the nation from atheism, the present-day threat. Much more than having God on our money since 1863, having God in the Pledge of Allegiance helps atone for the oversight of the framers who forgot the deity in drafting the Constitution. God in the pledge proudly proclaims our "civic religion." Religiosity is linked to citizenship, to the very concept of Americanism. Being a religious person is what constitutes for many the common experience of being an American. Newt Gingrich defined this civic religion best when, in introducing his proposal for a school-prayer amendment, he argued that it would produce "an America in which a belief in the Creator is once again at the center of being an American."

When the next Newdow challenges "under God" and it reaches the Supreme Court, as inevitably it will, the Court will not be able to avoid the constitutional issue on the technicality of standing. If the questioning of Newdow by Justices Souter and Breyer in March of 2004 tips their hand, the Court is likely to leave God in the pledge, holding that the pledge merely has school children mention God, not publicly pray to God, a practice excluded from graduations and football games. The reference to God in the pledge, they probably will hold, is not an unconstitutional school-sponsored profession of religious belief, but an incidental, largely secular citation of the deity in what is fundamentally a school-sponsored civic ritual that does not favor one religion over another.

Those of us who are Jeffersonian separatists live more or less easily with the accumulated chinks in the wall of separation like prayer at the beginning of legislative or judicial sessions, "In God We Trust" on our money and as our nation's motto. In remembering that Jefferson did in fact found human rights on a Creator's intentions, we should pick fights carefully and not ever imagine that references to God will or should disappear from public rhetoric. Removing God from the Pledge of Allegiance strikes some of us as not important enough, not as important, for example, as fighting school prayer. We make our own political calculations, thinking that purging God from the pledge would be a stupendous propaganda gift to the Pat Robertsons and Rush Limbaughs of the world. Nonetheless, if the Justices hold "under God" in the pledge to be patriotism and not prayer, then the Supreme Court of the United States will have certified and legitimized a civil religion for America, the idea that being religious, i.e., recognizing the existence of a deity, is part of what it means to be an American. This should be deeply worrisome to all of us, whether one be personally religious or not. The question of whether God exists or not is not a question that should be before our legislative bodies and our courts, whatever a majority might say. Besides, as in the case of the Ten Commandments, recruiting religion to serve a purely secular function for the state is no compliment to faith.

There are other worrisome examples of practices seeming to equate belief in God with being a good American. In their state constitutions, Arkansas, Maryland, South Carolina, Tennessee, and Texas make belief in God a requirement for state officials. This despite the fact that, as a matter of constitutional law, states are prohibited from having a religious requirement for public office. In *Torasco v. Watkins* (1961) a unanimous Supreme Court struck down the clause in the Maryland state constitution requiring belief in the existence of God as a qualification for office, which had prevented the plaintiff from taking up his appointment as a notary public. The Maryland requirement, the Court argued, violated Article 6, Section 3, of the U.S. Constitution. Justice Black, writing for the Court, made clear that states could not enact provisions that discriminated between religious believers and nonbelievers.

Since 1961, amazingly enough, each of these five states, including Maryland, have amended their constitutions several times but have not eliminated required belief in God from the documents. The force of the clauses may only be symbolic, but they do matter. They speak to pressures that weigh upon legislatures and to the mentality of those who appoint and elect people to office. They tell atheists not to apply.

When these five state constitutions were originally written, a common interpretation of "no religious test" was that a candidate for office could be any sort of Christian, even, with grudging assent, Roman Catholic. Later, "no religious test" expanded to protect Jews and members of other world religions. The possibility that nonbelievers were covered by no religious test clauses usually went unaddressed. Several of the states that maintain religious tests in their constitutions today follow the old rationale in maintaining that they do not impose religious tests because they do not discriminate against any religion. The Maryland constitution, for example, still reads "no religious test ought ever to be required as a qualification for any office of profit or trust in this State, other than a declaration of believers in the existence of God," as if this latter is not a religious test. In today's world it is an odd logic to say that the requirement that you have to be religious is not a religious test, that only the requirement that you have to be Christian imposes such a test. Yet, Tennessee in its Declaration of Rights, forbids religious tests for public office but adds the provision that "no person who denies the being of God, or a future state of rewards and punishments shall hold any office in the civil department of this State."

Only one state in the fifty United States provides specifically that no discrimination may flow on account of religious belief "or the absence thereof," and it is not any of the blue states from coast to coast thought to harbor large populations of "secular humanists." It is Utah, once denied membership in the federal union because of an alleged failure to separate its politics from the control of the Mormon Church. Historically the most persecuted of all religious groups in the United States, Mormons in Utah recognize that religious conviction or the lack thereof are not per se evidence of ability to handle state affairs wisely. They are, of course, echoing Roger Williams who is still way ahead of most Americans in taking religion seriously, too seriously to confuse it with affairs of state.

When it next deliberates on "under God" in the Pledge of Allegiance, as it surely will, the Supreme Court should clear the air about religious tests even if it upholds "under God" as civil ritual not prayer. The Court should find room to reaffirm its 1961 ruling, thus assuring nonbelievers that they, too, are American citizens who may on an equal basis with all others hold positions of public trust without swearing on a Bible or adding the line, required in some state constitutions, "so help me God" to the oath of office.

One final worrisome example of requiring belief in God as a litmus test for being a true American is the statement President Bush made when he involved himself and his office in the fuss over God in the Pledge of Allegiance. In the original political firestorm of June 2002, immediately after Justice Goodwin's ruling for Newdow in the 9th Circuit Court, the president noted that this unpatriotic ruling reinforced his commitment to only appoint judges "who understand that our rights were derived from God." This is an obvious religious test facing all judges who are hopeful for a Bush nod to fill a vacant Supreme Court seat. They will have to believe in God, the more publicly the better, and in God as the source of human rights. While nothing in the Constitution prevents President Bush from applying an abortion test for his Court appointees, requiring appointments to the federal judiciary to believe in God, even if it is in this case Jefferson's God, is an unconstitutional religious test. The president has taken an oath to defend the Constitution, even Article 6, Section 3.

Our argument throughout this book is that the Constitution created a secular state. It is a precious but confused legacy, one that Americans have fought over since the beginning of the republic. There is, however, some common ground. At the present moment no one in the country seems much attracted to the idea of theocracy. Americans can claim a consensus around the idea that government and religious organizations exist for different reasons. They also agree that in our ideal democracy the state and religion will not conflict and that each will work in complementary ways to lead us toward the creation of a just society. But the devil is in the details, and people do in fact disagree about how to distinguish the role of church and state and yet keep them part of the same public enterprise that the founders envisioned. Our argument has been that this happens in the most reliable way when we honor the formula "separation of church and state," an ideal in clear trouble.

We have championed Jefferson's metaphor not because it appealed to every one of the founders, but because we think it is a powerful statement about the need for a secular state and for churches that operate freely without any hint that the state controls their mission. It was not a throwaway line used by Jefferson to confound and embarrass his political opponents in New England, but a brilliant appropriation of an idea circulating in the best political writing of the seventeenth and eighteenth centuries. It is an American legacy that we ought to treat as precious, more now than ever before. At the beginning of the Republic most Americans, if they were religious, were some kind of Protestant. Now the religious landscape is much more complicated, and the sober reality that religion has been a key factor in dividing us into red and blue states cannot possibly bring comfort to anyone except political strategists who see naked opportunity in religious division.

We take heart in noting that Jefferson's metaphor has survived a long series of challenges. But they continue. Philip Hamburger, a legal scholar, has recently challenged the idea that religious dissenters in early America championed a full notion of separation of church and state and suggests that the idea only became popular when Protestant nativists became alarmed about the "Catholic menace" in the second quarter of the nineteenth century. The formula of church-state separation was a way to keep Catholics from building their own schools. In Hamburger's account, the popularity of Jefferson's metaphor, especially in the judicial writing of Supreme Court Justice Hugo Black, once a member of the anti-Catholic Ku Klux Klan, is little more than a way to carry out Protestant prejudice against competing forms of Christianity.

Scholars have gone after Jefferson in a variety of other ways. Critics of Jefferson point out correctly that he and his friend James Madison by their own actions proved that the idea of a wall, with no contact between religion and state rhetoric and policy, was impossible. After all, it was Jefferson who taught Americans that a divine creator was the author of human rights. If we wanted to keep schoolchildren from confronting any idea that a real God actually did something important for our democracy, we would not let them read the Declaration of Independence or the Virginia

Statute of Religious Freedom. Following this idea, some scholars argue that Jefferson's metaphor is premised on historical worries that no longer exist and that to continue the metaphor blocks valuable initiatives that might improve our charities and our schools. We face here a postmodernist argument that trying to draw a line between church and state is a pointless enterprise since lines that purport to make clear distinctions are unstable social constructions. Different people with different motives try to maintain the line in different historical periods. It remains blurred.

We remain firmly unpersuaded. Whatever nativist prejudices dictated the policy that public money would not go to religious schools, Americans were not merely expressing a blind hatred of Catholics. They were responding to the Papal pronouncements of the nineteenth century that were hostile to all forms of political liberalism. Whatever may be said in praise of Pope Pius IX, he was among a battery of European observers who hoped for the failure of the American democratic experiment. It was not prejudice but a determined defense of American democracy that sharpened American notions of church-state separation in the mid-nineteenth century. Ironically, under that sharpened ideology, the American Catholic Church grew and prospered as did almost all other forms of organized Christianity. By the end of the century, a number of leading American Catholics had become champions of Jefferson's metaphor, arguing, in ways not without merit, that Protestants were far more likely than they were to mingle church and state. They knew that American Protestants who were trying to pass a Christian amendment to the Constitution were even more anti-Catholic than the ones denying public aid to parochial schools. Historically speaking, religious minorities in this country have always sought protection in defending church-state separation. A continuous set of grievances links colonial Protestant dissenters to nineteenth-century Catholics and Jews and Mormons to twenty-first century Muslims.

Of course it is impossible to maintain an impenetrable wall in a country where sacred and secular intermingle at so many levels of culture. Of course it is unwise to insist on a tortured defense of that wall when sensible public policy demands that the state provide assistance to the charitable and educational work of religious groups as long as religious proselytizing is not an issue or not a significant issue. At the same time, we need a standard to guide our policy, a standard that reminds us always of what this country in its origins aimed to do and why that was important. If, in writing about the founders, we privilege Jefferson and Madison, it is because we think they saw further than many of the others. Their ideas about church-state separation, their anger at or indifference toward many of the defenders of the church establishment in New England and Virginia, were not far away from the ideas of the others we revere—from Washington and John Adams and Benjamin Franklin. None of them was an orthodox Christian, and all of them held religious views that would have put them into plenty of trouble in the 2004 election had they been running for office. To us, that fact is not progress either for the concept of tolerance or for democratic practice.

Not all of this book and its prescriptions are about the Constitution. Its chief concerns are the wise and unwise ways in which we allow religion to become part of political and public rhetoric. We have probably not repeated often enough our view that most religious Americans when they attend worship service are not seeking political advice or instructions about how to vote. The very idea is offensive to them. Nor does anything like a majority of ministers or priests or rabbis or imams make politics a part of their services. Religious Americans do learn about moral norms in their places of worship. Many sorts of religious morality, as in fact many sorts of secular morality, oppose sexual intercourse outside of marriage, homosexuality, and abortion. But that fact does not make American religions the source of gay bashing, or the primary obstacle to the practice of safe sex, or the breeding ground of abortion-clinic bombers. Religious believers in America are in general charitable people who give far more money to hospitals and schools and AIDS clinics around the world than people who have no religion. If many white male Protestants in this country are inclined to vote Republican rather than Democratic, it is not because most of them heard their pastor support George Bush.

In our opinion, however, something regrettable has poisoned American politics in the past fifteen years. Politicians discovered that religious people can become an interest group and started pouring money into campaign strategies designed to encourage people to think of elections as contests between godly people and not-so-godly people. Somehow it became an acceptable idea that political candidates ought to talk about their religion. It was not just the religious conservative who talked in this way, but liberal evangelicals as well. Jim Wallis, the admirable editor of *Sojourners* magazine who has tried to turn religion toward its prophetic role in peacemaking and justice seeking, urges liberals to take up God's politics, for Democrats to think of religion not as something private but as something that can guide their campaigns. However worthy the cause, Wallis is urging politicians to speak in the religious accents of the majority, in ways that only encourage the idea that America is a Christian nation. We are in full accord with anyone who wants to see moral passion as part of our political life. And we are in full accord that religious leaders have something valuable to add to public debate. At the same time, we think that we should do everything we can to discourage politicians from making their personal faith a campaign issue. John Kennedy was right. Warren Burger was right. When religion goes public and partisan, it serves no cause but division.

Many committed Christians are in danger of forgetting just how painful it is for non-Christians in this county to hear constant references to Christ as if Christianity defines our normative culture. Religious people of all kinds must always keep in mind that the United States and many of the countries that we must work with are filled with people who have no religion at all, that these people are decent, moral people who lead honorable lives of public service and who love their spouses, their children, and their grandchildren. All of us are in danger of imagining the wrong enemies. Secularists have nothing to fear from religious people who more often than not share their values. And religion has nothing to fear from secularists, who have hardly driven religion out of the American psyche. They have nothing to fear from feminists or gays who also want to contribute to the advancement of liberty and equality in this country. We all suffer from public rhetoric encouraging hatred. We all suffer from public rhetoric built on arrogance, the kind of arrogance that takes our eyes off of what are our common enemies: social injustice, terrorism, and everything that threatens to cheapen our democratic enterprise. We can hardly export democracy to the world when we have such trouble maintaining it at home. It would take another book to outline how much our commercial free press has added to our problems.

We can conclude simply. American organized religions have to this day prospered to a degree unparalleled in Europe. In England, our only close ally in our present foreign policy ventures, 3 percent of the population attend the services of the Anglican Church on an average Sunday. When asked to rank ten things important to their lives, 80 percent of the English put religion at the bottom of the list. Yet lively democratic debate goes forward in the House of Commons in ways that shame the American Congress. The English vote in numbers far greater than Americans. Politically the English are divided, but they do not quarrel about religion. For organized religion in this country to make itself the object of angry attack from half the American population, or vice versa, is dangerous folly. For every constituency in this country, for the people who believe in one god or twenty gods or no god, Jefferson's idea of the wall of separation between church and state remains the best possible metaphor to guide the American secular state. No matter how many times the boundary is crossed, no matter how many times Jefferson might have crossed it himself, it makes sense. The American Constitution, in letter and in spirit, must remain Godless, open to all religions and to all people who build decent lives without religion.

A NOTE ON SOURCES

BECAUSE WE HAVE intended the book to reach a general audience, and also because the material we have cited is for the most part familiar to historians and political scientists, we have dispensed with the usual scholarly apparatus of footnotes. We do, however, wish to acknowledge our most important sources, both to say thanks to our colleagues from whom we have learned and to suggest some books and documents that our readers might with profit peruse. We are both scholars who have researched and have treated, although in a different context and with different intent, in our other books much of what is presented here. Needless to say, any errors that appear are our responsibility. So are our opinions, though in this case we blame them on the two men whose names appear on the dedication page.

With respect to the question raised in Chapter 1—"Is America a Christian Nation?"—Jon Butler, *Awash in a Sea of Faith: Christianizing the American People* (Cambridge, Mass., 1990), and David D. Hall, *Worlds of Wonder, Days of Judgment: Popular Religious Belief in Early New England* (New York, 1989), provide historical background for the colonial and revolutionary periods. The most recent statements about the purposes of the Christian Coalition are (on the positive side) Ralph Reed, *Politically Incorrect: The Emerging Faith Factor in American Politics* (Dallas, 1994), and (on the negative side) David Cantor, *The Religious Right: The Assault on Tolerance and Pluralism in America* (New York, 1994).

Much of the primary material for the chapter "The Godless Constitution" can be found in the sixteen-volume *Documentary History of the Ratification of the Constitution,* ed. Merrill Jensen (Madison, Wis., 1976–). An equally important source is the six-volume *The Complete Anti-Federalist,* ed. Herbert J. Storing (Chicago, 1981).

One excellent study of Roger Williams's views on church and state is Edmund S. Morgan, *Roger Williams: The Church and the State* (New York, 1967). But there is really no substitute for reading Williams himself. A handy compendium of documents that deal with his views on church and state is Irwin H. Polishook, *Roger Williams, John Cotton and Religious Freedom: A Controversy in New and Old England* (Englewood Cliffs, N.J., 1967).

For the chapter "The English Roots of the Secular State" the reader should consult any standard work of John Locke's writings, especially his *Second Treatise of Civil Government* and *Letter Concerning Toleration.* Burke's views can be found in any of the modern editions of his classic *Reflections on the Revolution in France.* For selections from Priestley's works see *Priestley's Writings on Philosophy, Science, and Politics,* ed. John Passmore (New York, 1965).

Jefferson's writings cited in Chapter 5 and elsewhere in the book are included in *The Political Writings of Thomas Jefferson,* ed. Edward Dumbauld (New York, 1955), as well as in the *Portable Jefferson,* ed. Merrill D. Peterson (New York, 1975). Details about his life and beliefs are developed in two important biographies: Dumas Malone's *Jefferson and the Ordeal of Liberty* (Boston, 1962) and Merrill D. Peterson's *Thomas Jefferson and the New Nation* (New York, 1970). For views on religion and politics held by the other framers, the best sources are still Norman Cousins's *"In God We Trust": The Religious Beliefs and Ideas of the American Founding Fathers* (New York, 1958) and Edwin S. Gaustad's *Faith of Our Fathers: Religion and the New Nation* (San Francisco, 1987).

The towering scholarship about Baptists and their role as dissenters in colonial New England was carried out by the late William G. McLoughlin, for his *New England Dissent, 1630–1833: The Baptists and the Separation of Church and State* (Cambridge, Mass., 1971). Other valuable studies dealing with the politics of Baptists in the nineteenth and twentieth centuries are Arthur Emery Farnsley, *Southern Baptist Politics: Authority and Power in the Restructuring of an American Denomination* (University Park, Pa., 1994); Nancy Tatom Ammerman, *Baptist Battles: Social Change and Religious Conflict in the Southern Baptist Convention* (New Brunswick, 1990); Rufus B. Spain, *At Ease in Zion: Social History of Southern Baptists, 1865–1900* (Nashville, 1967); and John Lee Eighmy, *Churches in Cultural Captivity: A History of the Social Attitudes of Southern Baptists* (Knoxville, 1987).

Our discussion of the debate about Sunday mail and the Christian amendment has been informed by two excellent articles and a splendid book: James R. Rohrer's "Sunday Mails and the Church-State Theme in Jacksonian America," *Journal of the Early Republic* 7 (Spring 1987): 53–74; Richard R. John's "Taking Sabbatarianism Seriously: The Postal System, the Sabbath, and the Transformation of American Political Culture," *Journal of the Early Republic* 10 (Winter 1990): 517–67; and Morton Borden's *Jews, Turks, and Infidels* (Chapel Hill, N.C., 1984).

The arguments presented in Chapter 8 can be viewed as respectful dissents from positions taken by Robert Bellah, "Civil Religion in America," in Robert Bellah and William McLoughlin, eds., *Religion in America* (Boston, 1968); Richard John Neuhaus, *The Naked Public Square: Religion and Democracy in America* (Grand Rapids, 1984); and Stephen L. Carter, *The Culture of Disbelief: How American Law and Politics Trivialize Religious Devotion* (New York, 1993). The quarrels we have with many leaders of the religious right are sharper. We have culled many of their positions from the extensive media coverage (television, newspapers, magazines) it has received in recent years. Our thanks to a Cornell student, Scott Youdall, for helping to track down references. We also have cited from the following books: Pat Robertson, *The Turning Tide: The Fall of Liberalism and the Rise of Common Sense* (Dallas, 1993); Jerry Falwell, *Listen, America!* (Garden City, N.Y., 1980); and Patrick J. Buchanan, *Right from the Beginning* (Boston, 1988).

INDEX

"By writing an unusually forthright book, Professors Kramnick and Moore have ventured into a public square teeming with religio-political activity, and they are ready to meet the opposition head on." —Stan Lichtenstein, *American Jewish Congress*

"This volume will no doubt be welcomed by readers who are troubled by the resurgence of religion and religiously grounded moral judgment in American politics."

—Richard John Neuhaus, *Theology Today*

"A sound and spirited defense of the wall of separation between church and state. . . . A timely reminder . . . that even the touchiest issues can be treated with intellectual honesty and a decent appreciation for opposing views." —*Kirkus Reviews*

More Praise for *The Godless Constitution*

"Kramnick and Moore remind us that it took a great struggle for the framers of the Constitution and other early American figures to create a nation in which there was no religious test for office holding. . . . For the Constitution not to mention religion at all represented a rejection . . . an extremely controversial decision *not* to make the United States a Christian nation. It wasn't contemporary liberals who upset the founders' religious ideas about the United States, it was the founders who upset the Puritans' ideas." —Nicholas Lemann, *The New Republic*

"Persuasive and powerful . . . a book that is essential reading for everyone engaged in the never-ending debate about the nature of America's moral values, where they came from, and how we can preserve and perpetuate them."
  —Robert F. Drinan, S. J., Georgetown University Law Center

"Drawing on their combined professional learning . . . [Kramnick and Moore] marshal in support of their position the contents of well-stocked minds. And they identify the critical victory of Williams and Jefferson, reflected not only in what the Founders wrote but also in the unsuccessful, though robust, assaults by the opposition." —Marvin E. Franklin, *The New Leader*

"The historic irony which the authors of this book brilliantly illustrate and which is most aptly summarized in their title is that, of all the great nations ever established, the founders of the American Republic best understood the danger of mixing politics and religion, and deliberately devised a constitution which would forbid it, not merely then but in all future times of trial."
  —Michael Foot, *Evening Standard*